Antony Johae

Poems of the East

This paperback edition published 2015 by Gipping Press Ltd
Gipping Press Ltd, Units 1&2 Lion Barn Ind. Estate,
Needham Market, Ipswich, Suffolk IP6 8NZ

ISBN 978-0-9931108-4-9

First published in the United Kingdom in 2015.

Copyright © 2015 Antony Johae, all rights reserved. This book is copyright under the Berne Convention.

Antony Johae asserts the copyright to the collection of creative pieces as printed in Poems of the East and the moral right to be identified as the author of this work in accordance with the Copyright, Designs and Patents Act 1988.

All rights reserved. No part of this publication may be reproduced, stored in a retrieval system, in any form or by any means, electronic, mechanical, photocopying, recording or otherwise, without the prior written permission of the author, application for which should be addressed to the publisher.

For the members of the Kuwait Writers Workshop,
who came and went,
1993 – 2009

Contents

Introduction	1
At First in Kuwait (after Liberation, 1991)	5
Desert Flowers	7
Black Gold (after Williams)	8
Arab in a White Steed	9
Ode to an Iron Lady	10
Wings	11
Skating in Kuwait	12
Old Gods and New	13
The Path Not Taken	14
Al-Kuwaiti Brothers (for Yahya Taleb Ali)	15
Arrival at Rafik Hariri International Airport	25
Night before the Beauty Contest	26
To Have and To Hold	28
Not Far to Galilee	29
At Sheba	30
Later at Sheba	31
Rachel in Rafah	33
Looking Backward	35
Christ's Tree	36
Diviner	37
Anecdotes of a Driver	38
Lawrence at Wadi Rum	41
At Shiraz	43
Throwing Stones	45
Naghmeh	46
Mosque in Kabul – 2002	48
Mosque in Kabul: Epilogue	49
At Ayutthaya	50
Pantoun for Adeline	52
Trio	54
Philipina	55

On the Great Wave 56
Ode to Doctor Xiao on His Departure 59
Lines for Lina 60
Sonnet to Sister Sun 61
Precept 62
Dr Hu Chun Guang's Words 63
Dr Hu's Last Words 64
From Liu Lihui, to Her Daughter 65
Creation Story 66
Chinese Woman 67
Guardians to the King 68
Variation on the Tao Years (for Xiao Zhe) 69
Check Lists 75
Kamishibai 76
Music for Two Players 77
Tōhoku and Fukushima 78
Going Hawaiian 79
Forecasts and Outcasts 80
Instrumental 82
Airport Butterfly 84
Sheets 85
After Execution 86
Resting Place 87
Three Feng Shui Matters for Pinky Kapoor 89
Kumbh Filth 92
Tagore at Twenty-Five 93
Tagore at Sixty-Two 94
From Poverty to Palace 95
For Sunder and Guilaine 96
Nile 98
Hieroglyphic Picture 100
Pairidaēza (for Halim) 101
Sticky Fingers 102
Kuwait's Old Boats (for Claudia Farkas al-Rashoud) 103

iv

Kuwait Eclipse 111
Cultural Crossroads 113
Two Limericks 114
Animal Matters 115
Chivalry in the Age of the Chevrolet (for Nasser) 116
On My Way to the Bank 119
Siamese 120
Mass at Salwa 122
At Last in Kuwait 123
At Ortaköy 126
Coming Home 127
Acknowledgments 129

Introduction

My poetic "journey" began in Kuwait in October 1991, soon after liberation from Iraqi occupation and the end of the Gulf War. Some of the early poems in this collection allude to this; others evoke quotidian life. I spent eighteen years in Kuwait, with my wife and two daughters, teaching literature at the country's state university. During that time I helped start up a writers' workshop which, apart from the summer holiday period, met weekly for sixteen years. Nearly all the poems in this collection were written then and were critiqued by the group. I owe the members a great debt, particularly Sean Toner, David Underwood, Tony Nunn, Thymios Carabas, Staci Hobbet, Peter Kelly, Amanda Lotfi, James Stewart, Yvonne Pepin-Wakefield, Stephen Longwill, Khairunnisa Joher, Sanjula Sharma, David Oliver, Robert Morris, Nigel Llewelyn-Price, Paul Kennedy, Marjorie Mills, Tara Harold, Harvey Pincis and others too numerous to name here, bearing in mind the expatriate and mobile nature of the participants, hence my dedication, "who came and went." I am indebted also to my wife, Thérèse, my best judge, and to Rod Usher, who pushed me to publish and who put me in touch with Jonathan Steed of Gipping Press; and finally to Simon Parnell who saw it through.

In Kuwait, I was well situated to travel in the East; short visits to Lebanon (Thérèse's home country) were fairly frequent, and for this reason poems of Lebanon have been placed immediately after those of Kuwait. (At the time of writing, I am working on a separate collection for Lebanon where I now spend much of my time.) In close proximity, of course, is Palestine/Israel, and it is here that the politically troubled state of the region becomes evident. The "Sheba" poems mark the end of the Israeli army occupation of south Lebanon in 2000, while "Rachel in Rafah" was written a year after the American peace activist, Rachel Corrie, died in Gaza. Politics are also bound up with the upheavals of the region in "Al-Kuwaiti Brothers," a long poem in epic vein narrating the lives of two Jewish musicians whose journey starts in Kuwait, moves to Basra and Baghdad and ends in Tel Aviv.

Jordan, whose recent history has been affected by Saddam Hussein's Iraq, and the subsequent fallout from his demise ("Anecdotes of a Driver"), follows on from the Kuwaiti brothers' story. These poems grew out of a conference trip combined with sightseeing at Petra, and also my reading of T.E.Lawrence's *The Seven Pillars of Wisdom*.

While in Kuwait, Thérèse and I made a short visit to Iran at the time British naval personnel were being held there. Shiraz is only a short flight across the Gulf, but could hardly be more different to Kuwait both topographically and politically. We found it inspiriting ("At Shiraz"), disquieting ("Throwing Stones"), and culturally deep-rooted ("Naghmeh").

The two "Kabul" poems go back to 2002 when the Taliban were still in control in Afghanistan. "Mosque in Kabul" was prompted by an article in a Kuwait English-language daily, and the "Epilogue" followed on from a conversation with a student from Afghanistan who, as it were, supplied me with a verbal footnote to the article. The last line of that poem – "so too have the doves gone" – was later used as the title for an anthology reflecting on the theme of conflict (Jardine Press, 2014).

Moving further east, and based on brief visits, "At Ayutthaya" (Thailand), an imaginative ride into battle at Siam's ancient capital; and a Pantoun, a Malay poetic genre which has had few imitators in the West. These are followed by "On the Great Wave," a "big picture" poem capturing the tsunami that hit the coasts of Thailand, Indonesia, India, Sri Lanka and the Maldive Islands in December 2004.

The "Chinese" cycle originates in my association with doctors and nurses at a clinic in Kuwait where I attended as a patient for treatment in acupuncture ("Ode to Doctor Xiao on His Departure," "Lines for Lina," etc.). Resting in the horizontal for twenty minutes at a time, twice a week for several years, and often in conversation with the staff as I lay there, I learned much about Chinese modes of thought, particularly the importance of maintaining personal somatic and mental balance. These exchanges encouraged a wider interest in China, its culture and history ("Variation on the Tao

Years," "Guardians to the King") and its current position in the world family of nations ("Checklists").

Two of the Japanese poems derive, first, from the programme notes of a concert given by musicians from Japan ("Music for Two Players"), and in the second instance, from an educational magazine propounding the value of story telling ("Kamishibai"). A poem about the 2010 earthquake and tsunami ("Tōhoku and Fukushima") closes as religious allegory, and in lighter vein – "travelling" as far east as this collection sets out – "Going Hawaiian."

The poems located in India emerged out of two visits to attend the biennial conferences of the Shakespeare Society of Eastern India; the first took place at the time Saddam Hussein was executed ("After Execution"); Delhi and Kolkata newspapers provided ideas for some of the poems ("Forecasts and Outcasts," "Three Feng Shui Matters for Pinky Kapoor," "Kumbh Filth"), while others are recollections of the visits ("Airport Butterfly," "Sheets," "From Poverty to Palace"). The two "Tagore" pieces were written to mark the one-hundred-and-fiftieth anniversary, in 2011, of the birth of the Nobel-Prize-winning author and sage, Rabindranath Tagore.

The collection ends with a return to the Arab world – to Dubai for a wedding ("For Sunder and Guilaine"), to Egypt ("Nile," "Hieroglyphic Picture," "Pairidaēza"), and finally back to Kuwait with a celebration of bygone days of sail ("Kuwait's Old Boats") and to the modern horrors of driving ("Kuwait Eclipse"). There follows animal matters – cats, dogs and a special friend ("Chivalry in the Age of the Chevrolet," "Siamese"); limerick and anecdote, until farewell ("At Last in Kuwait"), a disturbing return to England ("Coming Home") and, in "retirement," vocation to full-time writing in Lebanon.

At First in Kuwait (after Liberation, 1991)

They put me in a hotel close to the airport.
From the enclosed room where windows didn't open
and management supplied the air
I saw silent cars cross bridges, underpasses
or curved clover leaf to join
a four-lane highway with large hard shoulder.
Further off, blocks reached up to a petrol pall
and unfinished telephone tower into the black of an oil cloud
aftermath of Saddam's sabotage.
With curtains buttoned back, an inside window
looked down on a foyer where post-war,
half-dismantled scaffolding part-revealed
Tuscan marble, discreet lights,
soft sofas, and flowers in vast vases.

In glass I dropped to the mezzanine
glanced through fingered magazines
thick with Dior, Givenchy, and Chanel,
eyed the guests lounging,
aproned serving girls – pretty and petite
the doormen dark
décor anodyne
and thought I might have been elsewhere, or anywhere
– at Madrid's Marriot or Houston's Hyatt
or Holiday Inn, Hilton –
but for my contract weighing on me
as I waited.

Then out of plush-muffled sounds
I heard a woman's cry reach to the roof
an ululation so profound
it moved me – to another place

distant desert in no city state
encampment, water-hole
men attired in white
children sandal-less on sand
black-covered women chatting
– and when I returned
there was a wedding party
making for a hired room
and all the while – at once rooted and remote –
women shrilling
for the sofa-seated couple.

Desert Flowers

In this dry land
Set between salt water and grey sand
It is hard to see how on earth
There could be soil enough for birth.
Hardly is there bird song in the morning
Nor does dew settle on the suffering
Surface. The long-dried-up wadi
Is charged with hot stones; rocky
Promontories punctuate space
And earth fissures home unseen snakes.

In the night it rained a rare rain
Saturated the land, cooled the plain
To a balmy brown,
Drowned the dry bed running down
Into the gaping fissures
Wasted, never measured.
Light saw where the water had gushed
Forming a fresh pattern of pebbles washed
By the torrent; saw the desert below
Altered magically to a carpet of yellow.

Black Gold (after William Carlos Williams)

so much depends
upon

black desert
gold

pumped into long
pipes

from dark oceans
below.

Arab in a White Steed

In antique vestment
He rides his mount
Power of horses at his foot
Round rein to hand.

With pressure
The steed snorts
Forward raising dust
On the watery way.

With glazed sight
The rider ups the revs
Steps on the pedal
Energy at his sole.

With purring voice
Without caprice
The white steed answers
The rider's throttled order.

Ode to an Iron Lady

Your name is Thatcher – Mrs
but we do not think this is
fitting. You are too strong to be straw.
Something sturdy is called for
like Black or Smith or Wright
matching your forged will to fight
Hussain's hateful hordes. Maybe
they're correct to call you Iron Lady
for you hit miscreants hard with your handbag
and with President and Prime Minister saw the enemy drag
itself back to Baghdad under
your steely gaze. Small wonder
they call you The Iron Lady, you
key leader, "liberator" at Ku-
wait's side, knight in armour who rules
with a corporal rod the fool-
hardy foe. We rise now in rare ovation
not Pindaric, nor Horatian
but in post post-modern mode
we offer this contemporary ode.

With best compliments from the Kuwait Aluminium Company

Wings

In the early days after Liberation
I'd take the omnibus to town
viewing *souk*s, eating *shawarma*,
buying silks for the absent women at home.
I'd wait at the stop in the melting sun
till the bus halted at my signal.
Inside, the air was unconditioned,
the seats like those on no plane,
hard and unyielding.

It jerked out joining fast cars townward,
picked up pace on the straight asphalt
as aircraft after taxiing thrust themselves down runways
before wheels leave earth.
Strapless, I hung on agape at looming flight
held tight the seat in front
the bus full throttle rising airward
passing over tops of flat blocks, crossing streets
with slight cars stopped in line at lights.
Headlong, it charged at burning blue
as though bent on fusion.
I saw the chassis crumple, the bus plunge seaward,
wings melted . . .

After flyover, it commenced
descent to a port of wide-bodied boats
where passengers waited at the Shuweikh gates.
Not long alighted, it took again to the tarmac
for take-off on short haul to the *souk* – my stop.
Airsick, I staggered up front to get off
and before the first step down
saw its plaque announce:
Midi Bus Ikarus Type 263.

Skating in Kuwait

You see them coached to spin and turn
to form fine figures on sharp blades,
girls with lithe legs and supple frames
taught by women who may once have reigned
on rinks remote as Rome, Rio and Kyoto.
These novices learn about the body's balance
bend of leg, stretch of arms
in practice daily on Soor's frozen water.
Here my daughter sprawled one melting afternoon
and I, old-jointed, joined her gingerly
holding fast at first to cool rail
while boys whizzed past on fast blades
like cars on Jahra and on Fintas roads
reminding me of Saddam's men who here
brought broken corpses to the morgue.

There's a local girl now taken by the ice
taking to it; she's seen
those skaters reach for the air
in figures of three, eight and Dervish whirls
and now she's out there mirroring their moves –
not fine-footed in loaned boots
with blunt blades and collapsed ankles
but elated , notwithstanding, arms
beating like wild swans
wheeling in great broken rings.
Only, not like them, she's in *abaya*[1] black
(no ugly duckling though), scarf-covered
imagining lithe glides, pirouettes,
three leaps, the bell-beat of wings,
her figure flying on ice.

[1] A black gown worn by many Kuwaiti women and girls.

Old Gods and New

You see them on the roadside,
wrecks left for pick-up to Jahra dump.
Ogun has claimed them – impacted scrap
satisfying metallic appetite.
He has mangled Mercury,
crushed little Colt, set fire to Gallant
and swallowed Swift in right of tribute.
His high season comes with the rains
for he is the first reaper
mocker of speed on slippery roads
shredder of expired tyres.
Dionysus is at work as well:
He has driven his worshippers to drink,
let them loose at the wheel
free to blunder on shifting lanes
before they go to the wall.
Such is the road to human ruin.
Rage draws some to warring Mars,
those who seeing red will stop at nothing.
Smooth Thoth too steals lives – from callers
who driving blithely find their numbers are up.
Chaste Artemis snatches at speed diseased,
those who at their desks know only sloth.
It is she who chooses them for final chastening.
All these lives are lost to diurnal sacrifice
oblations to gods of matter,
to cullers of friends, of families, and firms.
Is that why, as I cross the pedestrian bridge,
I hear in the muezzin's call to prayer
a plaintive moan?

The Path Not Taken

A Kuwait newspaper has brought out a booklet for the Holy Month of Ramadan. On its cover is a slither of a moon, various stars, and a shining lantern. Inside gives notice of the Month's meaning. We are told that it is not just a matter of "skipping meals," but offers "a comprehensive program for our spiritual overhaul." Believers "get busy seeking Allah's mercy, forgiveness, and protection from Hellfire." It is also a time when they turn to the Creator to be renewed.

Shaikh Ahmed Farooqi once said that the blessings of Ramadan outweigh those of the other eleven together. In tune with it, LG makes "shining offers" in the Holy Month: tall fridges on "easy credit" and Al-Wazzan, holding diet in the balance, purveyors of milk, invite you to "change your life style." Ramadan's rules of fasting follow: what it is, what its purpose, what validates or undoes it.

"Fast to be healthy," said the Holy Prophet – and here's advice on fasting foods and hard words for fast breakers; still more for feasters. Then on the back cover I see it: the figure of a man with white hair to his shoulders and a wide-brimmed black hat and read: "Live well on the way to an active life with quick-cooking oats by QUAKER."

Al-Kuwaiti Brothers[1] (for Yahya Taleb Ali)

In 1905 in Baghdad, a boy Saleh was born to Yacooub ben Ezra,
    migrant from Iran,
his mother of the Habbousha family, Lawi by name. Five years
and in the walled city of Kuwait, little Daoud was added to their
    number.
The boys grew and waxed musical; they'd take fronds from palms
and the hair of horses' tails to make stringed instruments of
    them
and plucking silently ape the *Bahri*[2] they'd heard the boatmen
    sing on Sharq's quay
as divers and fishers prepared to cast off or headed in with their
    hauls.

An uncle from India, come to trade, heard the boys in song, and
    visiting again
brought instruments for them – *kamanja* for Saleh, Daoud an
    oud.[3]
Custom had it that the fathers of Jewish folk passed down their
    music
to sons and daughters, but not so Yacooub his budding boys;
it was Khaled al-Bakr, mighty in music, taught them; he had Saleh
    playing *oud*
at tender ten with Daoud coming on apace. Young still, they
    mastered
the *Sout*[4] of Bahrain, of Yemen and Hijaz, played *Samri*[5] for
    Kuwait's grandees
at *diwaniya*,[6] night parties, marriages, and at festivals and feasts.
They sang local composer-musician-poet, Abdullah al-Faraj's
"I Swear I Loved Your Beauty" and had their listeners moved to
    rapture.

It was 1928 when ambition took them with instrument and song
    across the bay to Basra

where nights were alive and lucrative livings could be made.
Mohammed al-Qubbanchi, master-singer of *maqamat*,[7] heard the
 young men playing
and on night club stage, improvised with them into early
 morning.
Entrepreneurs heard them too, and cut records for new
 gramophones
in the bars and cafés of Basra and Baghdad, Mosul and Kirkuk.

Not long, and came a call to seek out metropolitan success; so the
 Ben Ezra boys
with father and mother removed north up the Tigris to the
 golden city
where the royal palace stood. Playing at *Malha al-Hilal*, a night
 club of distinction,
fame came quickly; they accompanied singers of note – Selima
 Murad
with Nazim al-Ghazli, her spouse (killed later in a car crash), and
 Sultana Yusuf for whom
Saleh penned record-breaking songs, known on radio from end to
 end of Arab lands.
"*Qalbak Sakhr Jalmoud*" –Your Heart Is Rock-Hard – was one she
 wailed
causing hearts to melt, tears to form; and when, in thirty-one,
 Umm Kulthum
came in cortège to pour out sorrow in performance, it was Saleh
 taught her
his troubled song, she who had spurned all but Egyptian
 compositions.
Zakiya George was another – from Aleppo, dancer at first in
 Ottoman-free Baghdad,
then singer of renown – to her Saleh passed on the magic of his
 music,
Daoud all the while plucking faithfully on five-stringed *oud*.

Then for Zohour Hussein (killed later in a crash) more songs
> composed,
Munira al-Hawazwaz too, and Syrian, 'Afifa Eskandar, follower
> of the Nazarene.
In summer season, towering Egyptian, Mohammed Abdul
> Wahab, took the stage
weaving his song to Saleh's seraphic violin and the harmonies of
> Daoud's *oud*.
After concert they'd exchange one *maqam* for another night by
> night
– the elder brother and Mohammed – their music and minds co-
> mingling
like alchemy into gold.

Tuned into *Zuhour Radio*, his personal station, King Ghazi heard
> the brothers play,
called them for audience to the palace, and so pleased with Saleh's
> songs
gave him as present a watch (was it gold?) inscribed with the
> priceless royal name;
then a proposition: the formation of a radio orchestra, under
> Saleh,
to serve the fledgling national station – an offer the brothers
> could not disdain.

This was 1936 with war winds blowing from the west,
Ashkenazim purged by Hitler's men,
and Palestine in protest at foreign settlement.

Interview with Albert A. Elias

– I was born in 1930 and studied Law at Baghdad University before emigrating to Israel.

- Saleh and Daoud had originally come from Kuwait and were well-known in Iraq for their music. They had been asked by the king to form an orchestra for the new radio station.
- Saleh played the violin and his brother *oud*. Yousef Za'rour played the *Qanun*[8] and Abraham Taqqu cello. At first the band lacked a flautist. "Why is there no flute?" asked the broadcasting director. "There is someone training," Saleh answered. "Bring him in! Teach him!"
- Yes, there was a Muslim called Husseinu who played *Dumbuk*.[9] The brothers wanted to show that the ensemble was made up not only of Jews. There were songwriters as well – many. I can't recall their names except Saif al-Din al-Wala'ee who was quite famous at that time. He wrote the lyrics for "Abandonment Is Not a Strange Habit for You." Saleh composed the music. In fact, he was the principal composer. Daoud was more an instrumentalist.
- No, they didn't write – they were poets already [chuckles], but poets did write for them. Saleh would choose a lyric, compose for it, and give the music to famous female singers like Salima Pasha, Narjes Shawqi, and 'Afifa Eskandar. There was also Zakiya George, a Syrian singer who came to Baghdad and was trained by Saleh to perform Iraqi songs. She became so good at it that audiences took her for a local. The association with Saleh became so close that Zakiya fell in love with him.
- They were together for five years, but in the month of *Muharran*,[10] when the playing of music was prohibited on the radio and at hotels, Zakiya decided to go to Basra to relax. Once there, toothache suddenly took hold of her and she had to visit a dentist. Would you believe it, she and the dentist fell in love!
- No, she didn't go back to Baghdad. Actually, one of Saleh's song writers disapproved of Zakiya's behaviour – so much so that he wrote a song for Saleh called "My Love, My Hope Was Not That a Third Would Join Us" [sings].

- During the time that Saleh and Zakiya were together, Narjes Shawqi – an Egyptian singer – fell in love with Daoud; there was an atmosphere of high romance at the radio station.
    "Well, well," the director exclaimed. "Has the place been turned into a whore house?" – and promptly fired the Kuwaiti brothers, telling them to "Get out!" That was in 1944.
- Yes, the band did keep going. Someone approached the director after Saleh and Daoud had gone – "I'll bring you top musicians" – and hired a flute-player called Shoua-Heskel, and a violinist to replace Saleh; his name was Sasson Abdou. Yousef Za'rour, the *Qanun* player, became the leader. That is how the radio orchestra continued – until 1951 when we were made stateless and came to Israel.

Ramat Gan, 8th April 2008

Prime Minister Nuri Said turning on his radio
found no music on the station, for it was *Yom Kippur*[11] – High
    Holy Day of fast.
Exasperated, he put in train the formation of a new orchestra
– Muslim Arab players only, violinist, Jamil Bashir, to be their
    leader, Ghazali to sing.
This was 1945 with unrest surging in mandated Palestine.
Three years on and a state for Jews declared in Holy Land
like the ancient kingdom of the Franj[12]
wedged between enraged Levantine neighbours and the wrath of
    desert kingdoms.
This making of an alien state caused displacement and collapse
    into statelessness
for many, among whom Saleh and brother Daoud set now for
    exodus to Israel.
The director of the station wept to see his leader go, pleaded,
    promised reinstatement.
But those that Yousef Za'rour loved had flown.
How could he stay, resettle and live alone?

Likewise the brothers who on board for take-off saw (or so the
        story has it)
black limousines burst onto the tarmac blaring: messengers from
        Kuwait's emir
bearing invitations to these leaveners of the region's culture to
        PLEASE COME HOME!
But of no avail in these hateful times – and with propellers
        whining, the plane, exile-full,
hurtled down the runway westward bound.

The good fortune earned in the golden city's clubs, cafés, on
        records and on radio
was lost to the Kuwaiti brothers – new-come refugees to Tel Aviv,
        once called Jaffa.
A man carrying a wrapped chicken would be chased from street
        to street
food being short in a country prepared for further war.
The brothers longed for the richness of their old life, would go
        back to Baghdad
had not all political doors been shut on them.
What to do but set up a simple store in the city
become vendors of sought-after household items
so that one of them could go on the prowl for black-market fowl
while the other looked after the shop.
But *oud* and *kamanja* did not stay in their lockers long:
at a café in Shkhunat Ha-Tikva musicians met,
Saleh and Daoud and those whose homes had been in Arab
        lands,
to play together, form new bands, these for parties, marriages and
        bar mitzvah,[13]
the hosts coming to choose their singers and musicians
among whom Moshi Mizrahi with voice like Farid al-Atrash of
        renown
who'd magnetize his men with uncanny imitation.

In the first years telephones were rare, motor-cars rarer.
Hosts would order taxis to transport their chosen players to their
       festive places
or they'd have to board last buses to Haifa, Hadera, or further to
       Tiberias
and play, like Cinderella, till twelve when the magic of their music
       was timed to stop.
Sleep then in celebrants' house on temporary beds
before day bus ride back to the coast and bland capital.
All this Saleh and Daoud did after *Aliyah*.[14]

In the kingdom of Iraq after the brothers unwelcome
       embarkation
their names were, by degrees, erased, their music purloined by
       Muslim singers
and when "Abandonment Is Not a Strange Habit for You" and
       others of their songs
were broadcast countrywide, composition went uncredited – at
       times ascribed to others.
Heard on Arab air the brothers choked at hurtful cheat,
they who had served the king, his flowering radio, and the nation,
loved the land where Tigris and Euphrates flowed,
who likewise were loved for the tender words they'd matched to
       music,
but since *Annakba*,[15] like "Your Heart Is Rock-Hard," banished.
Worse: in '72 with Saddam's rise, their names, by *decree*, expunged
from conservatoire curricula, books, bibliographies, and all
       records of the state,
their songs mis-labelled ex post facto, "Of folk origin" only.
But three decades and Saddam Hussein Abd al-Majid al-Takriti
       fell, was found
and died hanging with insults thrown, while Saleh and Daoud's
       songs enrapt in love
lived on in Levant, Gulf, and Nile lands, in far-flung *dar al-Islam*[16]
       of the East

and in Iraq revived, names reinstated, heritage restored, TV-
    featured, audience-favoured,
followed by awards – albeit the Kuwaiti brothers had
    inconspicuously passed on.

After Camp David, Mohammed Abdul Wahab, famed composer,
    singer of Egyptian stock
who'd once consorted after concert with the elder brother in
    alchemic composition
sent messages of fraternal friendship – not withstanding Sadat's
    stubborn stand-off –
to the new nation's major players, first among them Al-Kuwaiti
    brothers – Saleh and Daoud.
He'd heard them broadcast weekly on Kol Israel Radio live
drawing in the world they'd lost (palace, patronage, popularity),
and migrants, some like them, that rued the day of their
    departure.
But whereas in Arab lands their music revived, once more
    revered,
in their country of adoption those in high places pulling cultural
    cords
with uncalled-for arrogance ignored the Arab aspect of the
    brothers' heritage
confining them to an inferior foundry of Oriental melody, Judeo-
    Arab legacy disowned
while Occidental music swept up the charts of fashion
and Near East fast became Far West.

Epilogue

Among new-millennium Sefardim, cultural re-intelligence,
like light on new moon, shows slightly at first,
enlarged by time to a full sphere of knowledge:
wisdom, words and the melodic modes of *maqamat*
again fête festivals, feasts and large concerts
in praise posthumous to Saleh and Daoud's passing.

Just off Bossem Street in south Tel Aviv
on one corner a fine white villa;
opposite – large and neglected – an old apartment block
emblems almost of the brothers' fortune.
These now are found in eponymous road, newly named,
Rechov Ha'achim al-Kuvaiti – Al-Kuwaiti Brothers Street.

---

[1] My interest in the Kuwaiti brothers was first aroused in a lecture given by Dr. Lisa Urkevich at the *Dar al-Athar al-Islamiya* Cultural Centre in Kuwait. In speaking about the art of song in the Gulf region, she mentioned in passing a band formed by two brothers of a Jewish family, who had spent their youth and early manhood in Kuwait. This was before the beginning of oil exploitation in the 1930s, and when pearl diving and trading were the main occupations of the inhabitants.

    Much loved for their music, the brothers moved on with their parents to Iraq, where they gained enormous popularity both there and throughout the Arab world. I had not known that a small Jewish community had once lived in the emirate, and I wanted to discover in more depth and detail the contribution made by the brothers to its music and culture and to the wider area.

    An MA student of mine at Kuwait University, Yahya Ali, to whom this long poem is dedicated, helped me track down the brothers' history. To him I owe a debt of gratitude for the advice and support he has given me in the writing of this epic story.

[2] Maritime music; *tabl bahri* (sea drum), hence the song's generic name, *Bahri*.
[3] *kamanja* (violin) and *oud* (lute)
[4] Pronounced 'sewt' (pl. aswat), a "classical" song of the educated class: solo voice with *oud* accompaniment, and *mirwas* (small hand drum). Sometimes, also includes *kamanja* (violin) and *qanun* (plucked zither).
[5] Played at weddings
[6] Regular meetings, usually groups of men, taking place in a special annex of a private home.
[7] Arab melodic modes, with improvisation (singular: *maqam*)
[8] Plucked zither
[9] A small hand drum
[10] Arabic: The first month of the Islamic calendar, when fighting is forbidden. Some Muslims also fast; it is the second most sacred month after Ramadan.
[11] Hebrew: The most important of Jewish festivals; fasting is observed for twenty-five hours.
[12] The Crusader kingdom of Jerusalem
[13] Hebrew: A Jewish boy reaches religious adulthood on his thirteenth birthday. There is a ceremony and celebration.
[14] Hebrew: Emigration to Israel
[15] Arabic: Refers to the "catastrophe" of 1948: the declaration of the Jewish State of Israel, war between Arab and Jew, and the flight of many Palestinians from their land.
[16] Literally, "The House of Islam."

Arrival at Rafik Hariri International Airport

The queue wasn't long for foreigners;
the other for Lebanese, guest workers
home for a few days from the Gulf,
stretched back a bit. I stood on the yellow line.

He stamped the man before me
and beckoned. "Bonjour," I said and he smiled.
I handed him my passport, he flipped through the pages.
"You are coming from Kuwait?" and I nodded.

"What is your occupation?" "I teach at the University –
English . . . English Literature."
He looked at me and then at my picture,
again at me and said:
"Shall I compare thee to a summer's day?"

Night Before the Beauty Contest

We flew into Beirut on a warm June afternoon
friendly clouds atop the mountains, ready to rain on sea-facing
    terraces:
on sprawling vine, verandah plants, monastery gardens,
the courtyards of arched mosques, red-roofed villas and a myriad
    concrete blocks.
That evening saw a family reunite – after airport crowds – in
    upland home
to toast on toast drunk to a watered milk-white, until the sun sank
    into the sea,
lights came on in homely houses, and members lumbered
    ludicrously to their beds.

It struck in the night – might have been a sky bolt
but for no pre-emptive light.
Seemed more material than a god,
like some gross collision as cars hit head on
man made, not from the heavens.

It struck again with the family sleeping
no warning rumbling as might thunder
but an almighty crash as though God had dropped a giant plate
and it and the earth had cracked.

Curtains were drawn back, shutters raised, windows opened,
house lights and screens turned on:
tongues reached up into the night
smoke black swirled into the night
sparking timbers fell.
Metal melted and sunk on the charred earth, sprawled, grotesque.
Pumps screamed. Hoses spurted into the fork-tongued
    conflagration

ineffectually so it seemed by the camera angles, the panning and
    the zooming
as we sat watching regardless of sleep until light and screen went
    dead
and dawn spread over the mountains.

In the morning at Bsalim, fires out
wreckage only with small smoke still issuing
looking like an air disaster, this one, though, aerial bombardment
electricity station toppled, unmanned, made powerless by
    southern fighters
come to thwart border raiders in ugly reprisal.

The man's bold to introduce the beautiful
after the city's hit and curfew's signalled,
yet he's on as surely as soap –
spots on, sound on, on camera
his looks projected – via Star – to all points
and contoured figures up for the global crown
pacing long-legged, the boards
all illumination, facing the global gaze.
Blow your trumpets, players,
to these goodly models
who from the round earth's imagined corners
come to assemble scattered bodies
All whom the flood did, and fire, shall overthrow,
All whom war, dearth, age, agues, tyrannies,
despair, law, chance have slain.
Trumpets blow!

To Have and To Hold

"We have no oil, nor deep-down gas
but rather a dark soil fed by bountiful water
sprung from high mountains snow-carpeted in winter
flowing down to Bekaa's fields in spring – to a trickle in summer.
We gather in nature's bounty – cherry, plum, and berry in June,
and in July, melon, apricot, fig;
vine and pear and apple in September;
orange and lemon in December.
We ski on Faraya's keen slopes and swim off the blue corniche.
These are," he said, "God's gifts granted us."

Walking one morning on the mountain side, climbing a steep
          path,
an unfamiliar truck ground by in first, puffing out poison.
I grabbed my handkerchief and placed it over my nose and
          mouth.
The air cleared in the breeze and I went on with my climb
passing wild spring flowers – yellow, white, purple – set on fresh
          grass.
Ahead I saw the truck stopped, turning and backing into a bush
          beside the path.
I had not reached it when I saw the driver get out and up onto
          the back,
then lifting builders' bags dump rubble – tangled wire, cement,
          broken slate and tiles,
timber lumps, rotting cloth, cardboard soggy with dew, plastic all
          shapes,
drums of metal empty of paint, glass in myriad pieces, parts of
          pipes,
fractured guttering, and a cracked latrine –
on God's gifted green.

Not Far to Galilee

At Cana he made water into wine and with a word
revived the lord's son, feverish in Capernaum.

It is not far to Galilee from Mount Lebanon
as the cranes fly south after summer.

But now there's no gateway to Galilee,
no pass, no passage, no thoroughfare.

The border's barbed and Galilee's a no-go zone.
You can't even phone.

Would that he came once more to Cana,
filled water-pots to the lip

with wine, settled an unlikely marriage,
saw war's fever cured, the way restored.

At Sheba[1]

The Jew came to the border to meet those beyond the fence.
He was thinking it a time to talk,
a time to understand those others,
to face the men and women of the land of cedars
who at the wise king's request
had once given timbers to build Jahweh's great temple.
He in his skull cap
(as they might wear in mosque at Friday prayer)
they behind wire in another land
waving flags in ecstasy at his army's retreat,
yellow flags poked at him
ridiculing his too-easy peace, impotent
after two decades of unwelcome occupation.

What amity now was possible?

Thus much realized, he turned away
from the separating fence
the mocking mob
delirious jeers
resolved to come back an ageing man
white flag in hand
to cut through frontiers
rip up border posts
one day to let the people tread the hallowed land.

27th May, 2000

[1] On 24th May, 2000, the Israeli government pulled its troops out of southern Lebanon after a twenty-two-year military presence there. Having for so long been cut off from one another, Palestinian refugees in Lebanon and Arab Israelis (Palestinians) were able, with the help of Israeli soldiers, to communicate across the Lebanon/Israel border.

Later at Sheba

A sister has never seen her brother
cousins who know not cousins
families severed by zones, borders,
barbed wire, fences, factions, frictions,
fictions, fractions, imagination –
come face to face across a space
(patrolled by the soldier's of Jacob's children)
to stretch out hands
make signs of knowing or of first encounter.
Let faces tell of joy at sight,
of grief at someone gone who now knows no boundaries,
no spiked wire, no impossibly angled fence,
no no-man's-land, no no-go zones,
nor watch towers to beam out trespassers
risking blood to clasp longed-for family or ancient friends –
        instantly.

How might such boundaries be broken but in death?
How might discord be dissolved and long disputes be
        disentangled?

Now here's a fenced off woman who's given no offence
holding a ring invisibly against the blue,
and there a man with bulky bag held high in hope,
and child with toy who'd have his gift given
but for prohibitory barbed wire;
and here's a fresh girl armed with gathered flowers
throwing them singly into the soldier's space,
too light to reach the Holy Land.
Benjamin patrolling picks one up
knows such flowers from home hill slopes
before service called him peremptorily to border duty.

Seeing the girl's fresh grin, he puts his rifle down
gathers up the scattered flowers to give to those intended
one of whom with gift in hand passes him a parcel.
The soldier's crossing back to make exchange
and, seeing this, the crowd's crazy waving parcels and packets,
letters and notes, baskets and bags they'd have similarly delivered.
Now Reuben's going from fence to fence – a messenger –
and Simeon too with *ka'k* and festive cake,
Levi, a mother's jewel
and Judah Kodak envelope with pictures of family poses.
There's Issachar, down the line, stretching;
Zebulun grabs;
Joseph drags a trousseau trunk with brother Dan;
fingers seared, Naphtali lugs splitting supermarket bags;
here's Gad rehearsing the Arabic tongue,
and Asher exchanging Hebrew words
– all crossings and negotiations,
exchanges and traversals,
mixings and circulations
– Resistances!

16th June, 2000

Rachel in Rafah[1]

It is a sunglass day
with light harsh on the dog tags of uniformed youths
M16s
tank turrets
lone bulldozer
and young Corrie's watch-glass – with the sand running out.
It is she who is standing her ground
before a home to be flattened.
Earthmover.
It belches into the blue
into suburban quiet,
and on plated tracks treads to
her on mound, erect, ten thousand miles from mother,
conspicuous from the cab.
She can see his face at the window
young soldier at the gears
hoping for a week-end pass
thinking of the girl in his pocket – the one his mother likes –
and of a larger future
with this woman in the way.
He'll frighten her to make her move
with time to brake
miscalculate
and in the evening weep at his levity.
Or would he see her die
in duty's line
all-pliant to Authority
and having served as soldiers must
shrug away responsibility?
Or is his an obscured view?
Now it's one tread too late
the earth's moving

and Corrie's gone
lifted first
then buried without box
on a demolition job.
Storied houses are razed
dust's thick in the air
and when it's clear – ground zero:
prostrate concrete, frenzy of wires,
a wilderness without distinction
except that Rachel's there
raised in insurrection
her spirit risen
from Rafah.

[1] Rachel Corrie (b. 1979) was a member of the International Solidarity Movement (ISM). She went to occupied Gaza during the Second Intifada and joined protesters there. She died on 16th March, 2003.

Looking Backward

Seven Palestinian women selling crafted things,
making money for Gaza and West Bank children.

The first, little cards for all seasons
Eid al-Fitr, Eid al-Adha, Easter, Christmas.
"Greetings," she says, "to all people of the Book!"

The second, rugs made behind cottage doors.
"We weave the warp of peace
into the weft of progress." She smiles wearily.

A third, selling folk clothes, bespeaks history:
"Six decades of ignominious exile; time now
to gather up our people for the journey home."

There's a woman with a stand of stitched cushions.
She still hopes for a return to her father's estate,
to a hill farm flattened by occupation.

I move on to Nablus ceramics. "This clay
is in our blood," she says, "our people moulded by it,
while they are strangers to it."

"Two millennia gone, yet they claim title to our land,"
says a sixth, selling books. "Absurd!
Like this, we'd all be under the Romans still."

The last is a Christian lady who needles crosses
into cloth painstakingly. She looks at me and cries:
"They killed our Saviour, they killed our God!"

I settle for a title on civilizations' clashes and collisions.

Christ's Tree

In Matthew you said to the multitudes
Now learn a parable of the fig tree;
When his branch is yet tender
And putteth forth leaves,
Ye know that summer is nigh.
Thus spoken before Passover
I rejoiced at the good news.
But in Mark on Jerusalem way
Seeing no fruit, you cursed it
And next morning saw the tree
Dead from its roots – withered dry.
How could this be I asked
It being spring and nothing but leaves
For the time of figs was not yet.
What lesson, Lord, in this stricken tree?
If a parable, what the key?

Diviner

Once in the Kingdom of Jordan a certain man went from
          Amman
south to wild Wadi Rum, and seeing a wilderness
of mountains, plains and moon-dry valleys
leased a large slice from the state – inexplicably.
Ninety-nine years it was for water-lacking land
enough to make locals laugh at the madness of this city-slicker.

Then came oil-searchers with their drills
and, boring, hit on no dark liquid
but wonderful water in a deep-down sea.
Our diviner set about planting and sowing.
Green sprung up where brown had been;
in moistened soil, tubers waxed large;
tomato-red dotted the plain
and in fierce sun, water melons fattened.
Thus from enriched earth our diviner became befittingly
          enriched.

Now, in large lorries, they're taking pipes down to Wadi Rum
to lay along the highway to Amman.
They'll stretch hose-like north
bearing water of great worth
to town and village near and far
from Irbid to Aqaba.

Anecdotes of a Driver

He runs to Aglun, Jerash and Karak Castle;
to Madaba, Mukawir and Mount Nebo;
Dead Sea, Wadi Rum and Red Sea port of Aqaba;
but most to the world's eighth wonder – Petra
– ancient city chipped out by Nabataeans from red rock mountain
junction for traders in spice and silk – from Greece's city states,
Pharoahs' flooded land and the high towers of Babylon,
middle passage to Arabia, India, and far-away Cathay.
Adnan, our driver, takes us there on the first day of May,
Thérèse and I, to sun-burnt Petra – and it is raining.
Car wipers make an unlikely sight;
we sit and stare through wet windows . . .
walk giddily on slippery pavements
among the blue, red, and pink of plastic capes, yellow caps,
bright umbrellas and scarves of sober local colour.
Horses, snorting, gallop by pressed on by bronzed riders;
others drudgingly convey ticket-paying passengers to the gorge.
We pass through to tower tombs, obelisk and caravan –
merchants with their camels cut out in high relief . . .
to the royal tomb – The Treasury – face and pillars sandstone-hewn
portal flanked by Leda's double-sons
and atop, a male god – highest-flying bird.
Thérèse takes pictures of all these.
How small we are set against this ancient wonder!

It was a hot day.
His passenger slept on the back seat stretched out.
Perhaps he'd been partying, our driver thought,
up from Arabia to enjoy a glass, a willing woman, a dawn dance.
It is a three-hour run from Amman;
he sleeps all of them along the familiar desert highway.
"Sir, here is Petra," Adnan says pulling up.

The sleeper opens his eyes, sits up and settles his head-dress.
"Take me to the beach," he commands.
"Sir, there is no beach at Petra – it is an ancient city cut into
    rocks."
"No beach! *Wallah!*[1] Take me back to Amman!"

Adnan was a driver of lorries to Iraq.
In Saddam's day, he says, it was safe
but now he won't go; he fears the raids of road thieves.
Before Saddam's men marched into little Kuwait
he would wait three hours to cross the Jordan border.
Then with UN posts to pass, it lengthened to six.
He has a client, a London reporter, who wants him
to be driver-interpreter in Baghdad's green zone.
The money's good; he has a wife and four children;
but he won't – he can't be sure of coming back.
I witnessed something, Adnan says,
at a check-point. A driver ordered to stop
drove on – perhaps he had not seen the American soldier
didn't hear him shout – only his wife and noisy children.
The soldier chased after in his Hummer
went alongside, lobbed a grenade direct into the mother's lap
– exploded with baby in arms.
It wasn't real, a blank with a big bang.
I think of that family every day and the baby – damaged.

I recall complaints by a conference delegate at Irbid – a Mosul
    man
who before crossing to the Kingdom faced stiff quizzing
by a soldier – black US – with grizzly dog that growled.
The Mosul man was angry, too, at Maliki who'd sent his men at
    night
to take reprisal because he'd cast his vote otherwise.

Adnan speaks to us of Hussein's days

how he gave poor Palestinians education gratis
supplemented visiting Egyptians' salaries
sent oil free to Jordan next door.
I see now why his namesake, the Hashemite King,
took his side when the tanks rolled in.
But Saddam poisoned Kurds with gas, I say.
Yes, and who was it put weapons in the way?

and I am confounded.

---

[1] Arabic: Really!

Lawrence at Wadi Rum

Back from Aqaba after long camel ride
he climbed the gully to *al-shellal* [1]
crimson-faced cataract, long runners trailing green
over bastion cliff edge. He heard the rush of the fall,
splash of water in a crevice under overhanging rock
saw silver runlet issue into the sunlight
thin spout from roof fissure tumbling
with clean sound into a frothy pool.
On water-cleansed ledge he took off sweat-soiled clothes
thawb, bisht, shemagh, agal,[2]
lay them on a rock for sun to chase out thronging vermin
stepped bare into the basin
and lay there.
He could feel the moving air touch his skin
dark red water run clear over him
rubbing all war and desert dirt away.

Then came a ragged man, grey-bearded, hewn face and weary,
peered with rheumy eyes at this white thing splashing
like a bird in the hollow beyond a veil of sun-mist.
Groaning, he sat on the bather's laid-out garments
closed his eyes and muttered:
Al hob howa min Allah; wa aan Allah; wa na hwa Allah.[3]
By some acoustic trick of rock and pool
Lawrence heard him, stood up and saw a shepherd peering down.
It took tender words for the ragged man to rise
to let the bather cover himself and dress.
Wondering at the rough man's spoken creed
he led him along crazy camel-trodden paths to the camp
where his fighters rested, but could make him utter no doctrine.
Between groans and broken words he drank their coffee,
ate in the evening with them around safe fire,

late, rose painfully and tottered deafly into the night.
They said he had wandered for long, moaning strange things
not knowing day or night, unsheltered, untroubled.
They gave bounty to this afflicted man, he never speaking
but to himself, sheep and goats, and into the firmament.
Next day Lawrence rode on with his men to lay charges.

[1] The waterfall
[2] *thawb*: white long-sleeved collarless garment; *bisht*: robe worn over a *thawb*; *shemagh*: headdress; *agal*: black cord to keep the headdress in place.
[3] "The Love is from God; and of God; and towards God."

At Shiraz

Here, long before settlement,
Earth's plates shifted and crushed up great mountains
taking their timely shape from Caspian wind,
high ice, spring erosion, and the sun's cracking heat.
In more time, from human encounters:
hewers of stone, builders of pillared palaces,
makers of tombs cut into rock faces
engraved with rulers' epitaphs.
After Cyrus, Alexander, Seleucus and Ardashir had marked them
and passed, came nomads from western sands
to settle their message in Persian lands.
Ritual fires were put out, the dead parted from vultures,
years re-measured and peaceful prayers pronounced
five times from dawn till dark
towards Zam-Zam, Kaaba and Holy Stone.
Arcaded mosques with slim minarets went up
and palaces pink and purple
patterned with forms, flora, beasts, birds and people.
Rilled gardens were planned and planted
which after rain when rivers ran muddy
filled with flowers in the fresh breeze.
Crafted carpets took their shapes from them,
perfumes their aroma.
All these seem like signs of divine presences
as I walk with my wife in April sun
– essences of principled beauty
so overwhelming in the women
as to cause them now to be covered.
In Shah's time I gazed at them veil-less
caught in close-up on *Time*'s cover,
girls in spring so rare as to be recalled in fall.
Now in this garden I see stone stools set in pairs

where couples court touchingly
as once courtiers fashioned verse for their ladies
and ordered gifts of silver for them.
With Hâfiz's tight lines in mind –
ghazals laced in light love, luminous –
we walk arm in arm through long paved paths
I imagining you ever more beautiful
with head scarf-covered.

Throwing Stones

Her head, scarf-covered, protrudes from a heap of stones,
cheeks are henna-red, sin-coloured.
Eleven like-women and one errant husband
await the pile and throwing of stones.
This one they say is innocent but zealot knows better.
He'll not leave whores alive to render pleasure
nor let cowed wives fall to a tender touch
or have men treasure each other beyond decorous kiss.
No – he would rather see them pelted out of sight.

There was a man who looking up from writing with his finger on
        the ground
saw those with stones in their hands set to throw at a hapless
        woman
caught, they said, in adulterous, venereal act;
but he would have none of judgement and invited them thus:
He that is without sin among you, let him first cast a stone at her.
And they recalling their lusts and longings dropped their arms
and departed. Only the woman stood there still, uncondemned,
        contrite
while her saviour made further marks on the earth.

Naghmeh

They number seven: Santur, singer
Tonbak, 'Ud
Daf, Tar
Komancheh
fit for Rengs and songs.

Seven scarfed women play
modest music of the mountain folk:
dirges cut from hard lives
– from rock and snow –
or songs moulded for supple nuptials
after mountains have melted;
and compositions of the lavish Persian court
where kings once lay back and listened
in walled and watered royal gardens,
heard the dulcimer strike out
as Izeh's stone tells us.

The four-stringed spiked fiddle
underlays the Santur's mood
the bowstrings pulled
To G, D, A and E.

Framed drum, metal ringed
jingles to tapped patterns.

Of lutish progeny
double-bowled, mulberry hewn
Tar with plectrum plucked
by brass along a score of fretted notes.

And rich-toned chalice drum

named onomatopoeically:
"Ton": low centre stroke, "Bak": side high note.

The celestial instrument parent to Chinese pipa
sounds primordial, played with a pick in D or C
for dastgah and maqamat.

To all these Naghmeh sings.

Mosque in Kabul – 2002

There is snow on the mountain
and the rubble, once a city.
Trees are without leaves
and houses are bared of their beauty
mere stones, mere piles
as are stacks of arms
heaps of shot
or collected bodies after bombardment
when factions have faced each other
and the firing has stopped.

Yet here's a mosque that's whole
in the detritus of war
its twin minarets mounting to a stark sky
its cupola arched over the prayerful,
portal open to the faithful
for quintuple praise.
The fabric's not touched by shells
nor seems troubled by men's struggles.
Only the droppings of pied pigeons
on broad roof or dome
spot it, perhaps beyond element,
with a quintessence.

Mosque in Kabul: Epilogue

They feed the birds with crumbs from their tables
or grain from late-summer lands
gleaned before the plough sets in
– women whose eyes cannot reveal their sympathies
smoking soldiers lounging with their guns
children, newly walking, ecstatic at mosque doves
who coo before the call to prayer
in the yard before the building.
Thus the birds multiply as at *hajj*
when pilgrims gather at the holy stone
to touch the dextrous hand of God
so numerous as to form a universe
circling with infinitude.

But the Taliban have come to stop the waste:
They'll not let deprivation last
when there's food for base birds.
They'll feed the crumbs to those in unsafe shelters,
spare grain to wasting livestock.
They'll not let pigeons spot the Holy Mosque,
pests soiling the celestial.

Now no one comes with their offerings.
So too have the doves gone – without nourishment.

At Ayutthaya

I am a warrior mounted on elephant's back
        awaiting Burmese chargers
Come to sack our templed city
        'Baghdad of the East'
Where cargoes from Cathay are shipped
        up the Chao Phraya river
Ready for the westward haul
        to lands aloof enthralled
By subtle silk or cogent spice
        or the otherness of Siam's rice.

These are *Elephas Maximae*
        small-eared with flat forehead
Trained in the trickeries of war
        and battlefield manoeuvres
Who trumpet into action.
        I have followed my Queen on one,
Suryothai, who died in charge
        against our perennial enemy.
Then saw I our city –
        palaces, temples, villas, houses, hovels –
Lit and levelled on hot April night
        and torches brand bricks and mortar
With the date of our defeat.
        Then courtesans and courtiers gave up their jewels,
Merchants and musicians fled,
        left goods and instruments to pillagers
While Court dancers swam the *khlong*
        and fleeing singers ceased their song.

I hear smooth-bored musket crack
        smell the pong of powder.

I, swaying in war-wasted air,
        feel struck by Burmese shot
And – falling – envisage a hero's pyre
        my body burning in crackling fire.

I am a traveller mounted on elephant's back
        Spiked by brush-like hairs,
my Thai guide on the animal's neck
        Calming him coolly on the road
as fire-crackers crackle and explode.
        It's not done to vex the beast
but to celebrate a Chinese feast
        – The Year of the Tiger!

Pantoun for Adeline

The cinema your uncle owned
Showing those you'd not seen,
Fifties films, and sixties, and well-known
Figures of nascent nation's screen.

Showing those you'd not seen
You studied them at Island institute
Figures of nascent nation's screen
Marking every womanly pursuit.

You studied them at Island institute
Categories of virtuous and fallen women
Marking every womanly pursuit:
Mother, maiden, whore and heroine.

Categories of virtuous and fallen women
You found them fall into moral roles:
Mother, maiden, whore and heroine
Formed by call to new state's social goals.

You found them fall into moral roles
These filmic women of Malay Archipelago
Formed by call to new state's social goals:
Political parts cast at fledgling studio.

These filmic women of Malay Archipelago
You saw created, good or mired,
Political parts cast at fledgling studio
But traced something else desired.

You saw created, good or mired,
Women fitted into cultural mould

But traced something else desired
A voice that's heard, a sex that's bold.

Women fitted into cultural mould
Yet subtly subversive, not flat,
A voice that's heard, a sex that's bold
Not a venture to be laughed at.

Yet subtly subversive, not flat,
Fifties films, and sixties, and well-known.
Not a venture to be laughed at,
The cinema your uncle owned.

Trio

They look out at their audience –
Soun-Youn Yoon slim almost as her oboe
brought from Seoul
her dress rather as the piano's white notes,
one to be worn at first communion;
Sharon Eng whose Chinese forbears
once shipped to the Californian coast
fingers tight across the neck,
bow dangling,
her viola at rest against comfortable black velvet;
of the Sunda Isles, Ary Sutedja-David,
like a painter's poppy, in flared red
whose southerly smiles have travelled the Pacific Rim
playing resounding grands and tight uprights
uncommonly tuned
due to lax managers or ubiquitous heats
– and bow.

Philipina

Speaking of brakes and
tired wiper, he sees red lips
and deep down brown eyes.

On the Great Wave

They call it tsunami, like a quiet girl's name,
not shrewish like Kate
but soft as harbour waves
that lap at port quays; not awful as Kate is
siren of disaster, but gently strange
as Geishas are in dance and song
and in their gracious exchanges.
Not so this wave whose wrath was caught on camera
who from an earth tremor reared up to claim the land
in what might have seemed revenge; or was it karmic
        consequence
of the earth's degradation when fisher boat was thrown on land
and train was thrown off rails? Or Allah speaking
when mosques still stand and the rest is down? Or the Nazarene's
summons to care?

They call it tsunami when the great plates shift,
the ocean swells from floor to surface
sending waves – enlarged circles heading for land –
felt by far-fishermen as they pass under.

This fell on Acheh's archipelago,
on pear-shaped isle, on Thailand's shores,
on Coromande coast, and the ocean's atolls,
touching even Africa's rim after consummation.

On the beach not yet reached
there's a girl, Tilly, on school holiday
who sees with alarm the water pulling back,
sea bed opened to the sun
and understands from class what is soon to pass.
She runs to tell her mum and dad who, credulous of her
        education,

hasten with her to the hills
while others, warned, follow frantically.

But on many shores those unknowing
comb for crabs or lobster brought to light
concealed coins
pied plastic
the bricabrac of ages
grabbed at and rated
– blind to oncoming wall.

It is the day after Christmas.
Not now a supper to celebrate
but inordinate wave, massive,
lunges at the land.
It's stark storeys high
and rearing with venom
curled at the zenith, now untethered
to plunge

over sand, land, into
hotels, hostels, huts, hovels, whore houses,
blue pools, past gardens sunk and salinated
plots and lost crops
shacks shattered swept away in pieces
razed markets awash with items of no purchase,
floating wood hung onto in the dirty torrent,
vehicles swirl into frail houses
hit humans like stones at the Lord's first martyr.
The petrified, swept up like Lilliputians in Gulliver's piss,
grab at the wave's floating detritus
or flounder in the swell;
children are snatched from their clinging mothers,
the inundated old resigned to the last;

divers are caught at snorkelling
bazaar baron – once a bully – drowned;
five-star cook, preparing breakfast, caught,
guest in self-catering, water at his chest
trapped in a chalet, flood at his neck,
but with weight against windows
hears glass explode
– and water recedes to the relieved man's knees;
there's the baby swept along in her cot, like the bulrush child,
dry as a boat until strangely found in a rubble of ruins.

All this in a so short time
unprepared for; no Ark made ready
for the deluge; no couples kept
nor any arc after in the blue, blue sky;
just hopeless havoc
ubiquitous swash
grotesque wreckage
dead flesh mire-covered strewn like shot soldiers after battle,
the still living waiting, like war-wounded, to be rescued.

In the aftermath, bodies fill the floors in sacks.
Medics in masks bend over the living.
Children sit and lie empty-faced.
Women weep as men search among the bodies.
They do not find. There are pictures on walls
with names and numbers written under them.
Those who pass by have not seen this one, nor that.
The faces smile out; they receive no smiles back.
Above them, a sign suspended near-illegibly askew:
Happy New Year.

Ode to Doctor Xiao on His Departure

You know of the meridians – qi's pathways;
Of the lungs' stations: Zhonfǔ, Yúnmén, Tianfú
To Shàoshāng;
Heart's progress from Shídòu to Shíxuan
Where the little finger is.
You know the lines of bladder, spleen, and liver,
Triple Energizer, Pericardium, intestines large and small;
The points – one called Extraordinary – another Governor vessel
– and again Conception.
You know these like the latitudes and longitudes captains go by.
They are the body's charted channels.

Once instruments were wrought in arrow-headed stone,
Later, needles cast in bronze,
Now steel to puncture temples and cut out flagrant pain,
In wrists and toes at points which hurt when pressed,
Abdomen from where the sun sends out its thousand rays.
All this for the servant and the guard
To preserve Yang's upward motion and Yin's descent
Outside and in, cool and passionate, energy and substance,
Opposites in complement whose lost balance lays one low.

But you go now to a northern place in winter
To Jilin City where a wife awaits you,
To a host of patients whose pain you'll expel
By moxibustion or the needle.
You'll not rest as we do here
Nor have time to talk as we have done
Of the world's woes, friendly food, meditation on moon and sun
I lying on clean sheets
While you watch over me.

Lines for Lina

When I hear the clink of your tray
I know you are coming with
swab and forceps
to pull out the needles
and wipe the pin-pricks clean.
Then you'll say sweetly, "Finish!"
and I'll rise from the bed,
but when my feet touch the raw floor
you'll be gone to another room
with a pouch of new needles, ready
for a waiting patient,
and I'll not see you even to say so long
till the next time you stand by.

Tomorrow will be a final farewell
to you who have pity for the poor,
a valediction forbidding mourning
for you'll be returning to old Cathay
to tend your own people, to help in their healing;
to home and husband
and school child who foresees your coming
joyously after a lasting absence.

Here, Lina will be lacking;
They'll be lean times for clinic porters;
Her particular lineaments too will be lost
to those in treatment, her leaning towards them
with cleansing lint remembered only.
These lines are meant to celebrate her stay
To last long after she's gone away.

Sonnet to Sister Sun

Your name means small boy to Cathay's people
Though to my ear it comes as Soon.
I think shortly you'll lie for care
Doctored by Hu's sweet needles.
Then you'll have done with smart and ache
And stand anon by fresh patients'
Pain.
To mark you is to look on the Sun
Inscribed; to wonder at your eyes,
Their light, their pull and passion;
Would you that sun begat son?
Or rather sit cross-legged beneath a Bodi tree
Sunk in serenity
Painless?

Precept

The first is not to take life,
That is, the Buddhaghosa says, from all generation.
Blameworthy are those who kill great beasts
With large effort, the small less so.
Does my namesake, then, bear little sacred weight?
These soldiers and workers, builders of colonies?
And the moth in my brother Tim –
Is his leaning towards light meaning-less?
The promise of his chrysalis an empty apparition only?
You say large matters; elephants then rise high in the scale
Though that mid-creature kill him lightly for his teeth.
And is the giraffe's stretching a sign of celestial zest?
You keep repeating: "Fare lonely as rhinoceros,"
Be want-less in the world, do not crave, cut out love and hate,
Play, pleasures, pomp, greed, guile and grudge,
Only fare lonely as rhinoceros does.
How can size be just when cuckoo, nurtured by small warbler,
Rules, parrot apes and peacock's known only for his plumage?
What of wren, tit and swift – trimmers of pests –
Or dove of mourning, peace and love?
I will cut this precept down to size.

Dr Hu Chun Guang's Words

As I lie at the open window
Hot wafts meeting treated air
Your needles linking Yin to Yang
My breathing long and Buddha-like
I hear you reading from a Chinese book
English in deep voice
Morphemes stressed both fair and false
With sense enthusiastic to come out
Found full in deep unconscious store
Travelling traces of the brain
Needing no resort to pool of signs
Computed and made plain on slender screen
But caught like webs on morning walk
Touching you with enlightenment.

Sometimes, though, you stop to ask me
Meanings – and I synonymise
Or sound out models to be followed
And you, content, continue.
But at others I find no phrase to suit,
Am lost for word, cannot dredge it up.
You take out your box-lexicon
And tap in Roman letters to my slow spelling.
I see your look from where I lie, expectant
In the crossing to your fond home tongue
In search of sense in Hu Shih's form
Pai-hua copied in six thousand characters.
And when it passes and the word appears
I see your face translated into wonder.

Dr Hu's Last Words

You said not to hate winter –
to put up with shivering showers,
to relish churlish winds,
stand up to influenza's grip,
feel free in trussed up clothes
– you said not to hate a thing.

This summer camping in Calais –
rain rattling on the van roof,
west wind funnelling furiously
down the Channel, I leaning into it
as I went to get fresh bread for breakfast;
and on Flanders roads, the sight of my umbrella
soaked lying on the van's rusty floor,
the sound of wipers wearing down,
and through the glass the constant grey of flat sky
– how I loved everything!

From Liu Lihui, to Her Daughter

I think of you, Yixuan, so far –
as far as Li Po's merchant went from Ch'ang-Kan
down the Ch'üt'ang to follow his trade.
I wait like the river-merchant's wife for her lord,
she who desired her dust to be mingled with his.

I think of you, Yixuan, so fair
in Jilin's summer, flourishing, my Flower,
among school children in some pleasant leisure garden;
or floats into mind a worry – Ts'ao Chih's petals falling
into fountain water, clinging yellow to the stone.

I think of you, Yixuan, so fine –
slender, keen, exquisite as Su Shih's seven-word lines
of thought written for Sung's imperial and cultured court,
or like Ts'ao Chan's dream, imagine you unreined in cloud,
running to me, rising beyond a temporal plane.

Creation Story[1]

It began as an egg –
the universe enclosed in a shell.
Then it split;
above became sky,
below became earth.
As the sky rose
and the earth thickened
P'an-ku, primeval man, came out
daily growing taller.

But P'an-ku died,
parted like the universal egg.
His head became the sun
blood, rivers and seas
his hair dark forests
perspiration rain
breath the wind
voice thunder
his fleas mankind.

---

[1] I took this Chinese creation story as a way of saying that man means no good. But a Jewish friend sees it differently; she interprets the images as the smallness of humans set against the greatness of all nature. She writes: "I don't think the Chinese, especially Buddhists, would see anything despicable about a flea!"

Chinese Woman

In the shop we talked
she on one side of the desk
I on the other.
I didn't see her stretch out her hand
to touch mine. She saw my surprise
and withdrew it.
Her features handsome,
she had once been beautiful.
He remembers the oval of her face
black hair swept back
and her faint complexion.
On impulse he returned her touch.
"We can go upstairs," she said.
He remembers the wooden steps that curved,
the sound they made as she went
. . . the early morning birdsong as he woke up.

Guardians to the King

They found them, terracotta figurines, in pits on Shizishan Hill –
horses, drivers of chariots, warriors lined up in their thousands
as though about to charge; and at Wanzhai tomb helmeted
        soldiers
in square-toed boots, with gripped shields, swords, spears,
        halberds,
crossbows, battle-ready for Xuzhou's twelve kings.
They dug down to a five-storey palace with vaulted ceilings,
to passages of tombs, a coffin chamber, stable, armoury and
        treasury,
cook-house and baths; uncovered a leopard in stone, gold belt
        buckle
with animal figures fighting; wine cup and burial suit in jade
made in multiple small pieces, gold-threaded.
At Beidongshan Hill, high officials – Confucius-wise – stand tall,
sceptred and black-hatted, guardians of learning,
bearers of merit, their stamp of authority bronze-sealed.
For the king's delight, musicians at Tuolanshan Hill
hair care-coiled, gowns high-coloured,
poised to play bamboo flute, silk-stringed zither and chimes of
        stone
– and dancers projected onto castle wall in billow-sleeved
        brilliance
silk shaped by motion, bodies swayed to music,
swirling as water from Hwang-Ho's slopes
sweeping like spirit air of after-life
a blossoming to pleasure soul
– all this ritually in Han's long dynasty.

                              Colchester Castle, 20th September, 2008

Variation on the Tao Years[1] (for Xiao Zhe)

1

How long ago it was that the Deity measured time!
He had taken the moon's twelve cycles as mensal count
but knew not how to name the advancing years.
After the Earth's fauna he thought?
I'll ask the other gods in conference.
"An animal race," suggested one.
"He or she who reaches Kumlun Mountain first
should bear the year's name; likewise those that follow."
Delighted, the Deity agreed.

2

Rat and Cat had long been friends (or so Cat thought)
but when Rat arose in first light for the race
he left Cat curled up sleeping in oblivion.
This rotten rat, determined to be first, crept away
and dumped his friend like a doomed ship.
Ahead he saw the profile of an ox with bent-back horns
charging war-like for the mountain.
I'll mount him Rat thought and dashed for Ox,
jumped up and rode him like a horseman for the line.

3

There's a gate of gold on Kumlun's height – entry into paradise
where Ox has come with Rat on top, both set on being first.
With tail high Rat drops down and scampers past the portal
leaving cheated Ox a sweating second best.

But he's a patient beast, emasculated, attuned to exploitation,
treader of the land, plough-pulling for the furrow,
heaver of heavy cart when the rice is gathered in.
Ox is not a bothered runner-up; content to be in paradise
he's not looking for a run-in with little Rat.

4

But imagine Cat's fury when she woke and shook out her sleep!
Rat could never be her friend again; chastened she would forever
    chase him.
Cat told her cousin Tiger her tale who, family-proud, raced after
    Rat.
Third past the gate, Tiger prowled around paradise in pursuit,
commanding those who lived there to beat Rat to bits if they
    could;
but heaven's not a place of punishment where the biter is bitten.
And so, Tiger, feeling the peace of paradise envelop him
settled down at Ox's side in a comfortable juxtaposition.

5

There's a corner in the wood where Rabbit and Turtle once met;
they agreed a race. You'll know that Rabbit rested while Turtle
    triumphed.
In bad faith the rodent addressed the Deity saying:
"I have worked hard. Should I not be the first-named year?"
Came a reply out of the sky with a note of annoyance:
"You are fresh – go now to the gate at Kumlun and you will be
    fourth."
Rabbit could not believe her ears and started crying tears –
    bucketfuls –
No wonder rabbits' eyes are forever red!

6

Now here's Dragon, a complicated character, who flaring up
on his way with Snake to the golden gate,
breathed fire into the forest to make a path,
Snake slithering along in the cool undergrowth
vain and high-tempered too, forked-tongue flickering
determined to be fifth even if by the skin of his teeth,
but Dragon – red with rage at his rival– took wing into the blue,
perched atop Kumlun, a scaly guardian at the gate,
like the armoured treasurer he had been before this race
– thus Snake slunk in sixth.

7

On the way to the mountain there's a tomb by the roadside
but for reason unknown Horse shied away from it, snorting.
Could he have hallucinated one wonders?
Or might the misplaced tomb have presaged a fatal fall?
Be that as it may, Horse stopped to put blinkers on
and with eyes so covered he passed by the treacherous tomb.
Horse may be the fastest domesticated animal on earth
but in this race, driven to stop by fear,
he galloped past the gate-post an unexpected seventh.

8

This sheep has horns and lives on mountain sides,
keeps warm in wool, likes anonymity, and a sparse subsistence.
News of the annual race came late to him in his isolation.
It was the forest deer who tipped him off – a dear thing to do –
and she and Sheep set off a twosome on a tragic trajectory,

for, you see, they met with a lake so wide there seemed to be no
    other side,
found no boat to hire or purchase, waded in till hoofs did not
    touch bottom
and started the long swim across. Alas, in the middle, Deer
    floundered
and went down! Sheep did not follow her to the bottom
but swam on smoothly for the shore, holding out for the
    mountain.

9

There were three animals particularly late for the race:
Monkey, Cock and Dog. Why this was so you are about to hear.
There was a man in Japan called Taotailang, haunted he thought
by a set of ghastly ghosts, spirits of the dead he hoped
had given up the ghost, he having chastised them in life.
Along telepathic waves, Monkey chattering on China tree-tops
and swinging from high branch to high branch, as intellectuals do,
got wind of Taotailang's torment and quickly called Cock and
    Dog.
Next day they took passage across the therapeutic Yellow Sea.

10

For therapy was needed to ease the man's ghostly guilt.
Monkey taught him not to give a monkey's for ghouls;
Cock's tale too was edifying, conscience not warranting the dog-
    house, he said,
to which Dog nodded. And so Taotailang, looking smart, saw the
    spirits off;
time then for Monkey, Cock, and Dog to push out the boat and
    head for China.

To Tsingtao they came, heard the news, and set off fast for the
		holy mountain.
Monkey swung post-haste through the forest, left the others
		standing
and landed, acrobatically, ninth-past-the post.

11

It is true that the cock has wings though they're not for flying;
It is true he's the first to crow before the dawn chorus,
but at cock-shut, when penned in with the hens, workaholic,
he's not used to flights of freedom or foraging in foreign parts.
So you're a cocky tenth – there's something to crow about!
Now what's happened to Dog? He can run fast if he wants
but his head's down on a bone a butcher dropped from his
		basket.
Don't blame the bone if he comes in eleventh – blame the
		butcher!

12

You've heard of the proverbial pig whose reputation is
		gluttonous and lazy.
In point of fact he had built himself a huge house single-
		handedly,
so not lazy but exhausted by labour – small wonder a huge food
		intake!
It comes as no surprise to find him sleeping solidly from Sunday
		to Saturday
and when he wakes he's not aware of any annual contest, that is
not until saucy sparrow, singing on window-ledge, twits him for
		his sloth.

Thus abashed, Pig picked himself up and, opening his door to a
    beautiful day
set off on his way to Lâo Tze's gate – so Pig arrived twelfth and
    last.

Epilogue

The Deity travelled Cathay's coast, along rivers and tributaries,
passed over its plains, forests, its deserts and downs, reached
    Kumlun peak
and well pleased with the new nomenclature, closed the golden
    gate.

---

[1] During my time in Kuwait, I befriended a Chinese doctor in Traditional Medicine who practiced acupuncture at a Chinese Clinic. While undergoing treatment myself for periodic headaches, Dr. Xiao Zhe sometimes had time between patients to enlighten me about his culture, particularly its more traditional aspects. When the Chinese New Year came around, I was intrigued to learn about the formation and naming of the twelve Tao years. When Dr. Xiao narrated some of the folk-tales associated with them, my imagination was set free to create my own sequence of brief stories to account for the "derivation" of the cycle's nomenclature; hence, "*Variation* on the Tao Years." I start off with a traditional tale as told me by Dr. Xiao, but then go on my way using my own fantasy with the remainder of the stories.

Checklists

Ordering his Chinese checklist, prelude to Hu's state visit,
President of the States must decide if payment to Gates
for rifled MS Windows, to Pfizer for imitation drugs
be prioritised according to patent; ponder also stolen CD songs
and DVDs of Fox's filched films covered by copyright.

Hu Jintao may have his wish list: tax on Cai Lun's sun-bleached
        paper,
on Bi Sheng's ancient printing apparatus, and Wong Chong's
north-drawn needle set down by Shen Kuo in Dream Pool
        Essays.
Fourth of Cathay's great inventions, solutions for gun powder
found in ancient army manual, proscribed in Chairman Hu's new
        peace.

Kamishibai

The storyteller comes to the village on his bike.
He has taken a small platform off the back,
story cards and big pictures. The sound of his clappers
wakes the village up from its stillness.
The children come out eager for another episode;
they crowd around the storyteller who sells them sweets;
those that buy the most may sit closest
to hear his tales. He tells them in
pictures, gestures and voices on a set up stage
about Peach Boy and The One Who Drew Cats.
He'll not end till at turning point
when ogre has spit Little One-Inch out
he's palmed these sweet kids in his truths
and they – alert for the rest – come back
to follow the story to its resolution
with Little-Inch restored to marriageable size.

Then came TV in post-war times to Japanese villages;
no bike now, no sound of clappers, nor street stories,
but soap serials beamed from far places
to children – PC sitters, CD listeners, DVD watchers,
Xbox players, Twitter chatterers, and cell-phone cyborgs
– indoors.

Music for Two Players

In Tsugaru the snow falls on heavy winter
Cold fingers pluck shamisen's three strings
Its sounds are at once tenacious and tender
They tell of blind wanderers who play at home doors
Lending sight to spring
Picture cascading streams
Fresh green freed from frost
And the blossoming of cherry trees.

In Tsugaru the sun heats red-chimneyed roofs
A drum beckons summer celebration
Light taps are made lazy by blazing days
Intermittent like distant gunfire
In hot battle. First *Jonkara*
Telling of temple priest braving cruel disgrace
At a rival's grave, punished by lord of war
Driven to river's edge, to self-immolation.

Then *Aiya* brought by shippers and fishers
A southerly song for shifting workers
Now heard at Tsugaru parties
Sung with light spirit on white nights,
And long *Yosare,* intricate, woven
Of tight-stringed highs falling to open notes
Seeming to die in their deepness
While vowels bend like late flowers towards Kyoto.

Tōhoku and Fukushima

"The happiest man is he who learns from nature the lesson of worship." – Ralph Waldo Emerson

For six minutes underwater the earth shook
east of Tōhoku's peninsula.
Then came a great wave,
rushed high towards Honshu,
swept envenomed ten miles across the land.

Fukushima Daiichi could not stand in its way
its paltry walls overrun,
systems swamped.
Came untimely explosions
and outpourings of fear
hot reactions let into the air
and into the teeming ocean.

Six feet the deep bed dropped in a seismic epileptic second
bred enough to power Osaka or Nagoya for a year,
a bolt six hundred million times ill-fated Hiroshima.
In this wise, tectonic plate shifted four score feet towards Tōhoku
Earth's axis altered
its tilt
rate of rotation
diurnal circle micro-seconds shortened.

If this be allegory
let Fukushima's plant be man's high hubris,
Tōhoku's motion, Heaven's wrath.

Going Hawaiian

After the great wave hit Fukushima Daiichi and plant shut down
Tokyo found itself for hours power-starved and in the dark.
Shintaro Ishihara, city governor, called for drinks to be cooled
in home fridges, slot vendors unplugged.

Bosses of stretched businesses ordered a dimming of lights,
warmed toilet seats switched off,
AC levelled to near-summer heats;
advised shirts short-sleeved, trousers cotton
and open footwear at the work place
(but not ultra-casual shorts and thongs).

Accustomed to a suited dress code
office workers arrived at first with caution
pressed jacket on arm and sober tie in polythene pocket
in case called out.

Not so now in Tokyo's commercial quarter
– on Friday they all go loud Hawaiian.

Forecasts and Outcasts

Another bright and sunny day . . .
It was supposed to be the coldest, but wasn't.
Now it's hovering around the normal mark
at 6.3 degrees: simple winter minus fog.
Thus spake the duty officer at Safdarjung Met Office.

At Indira Gandhi International Airport, R.K. Jenamani
Director at IMD Office, also has warm words:
No more holdups, backlogs are dealt with,
the disturbance from the west is gone,
no possibility of thick fog
no high moisture – a measly 36 degrees.
And there's a north-westerly blowing,
the chance of a foggy tomorrow is bleak.
There's a thin layer still, but all right for flights.
On Thursday it will be shallow
the runway range will be comfortable.
Friday will be fogless with one degree warmer.

. . . but no respite for destitutes,
for beggars, contract labourers, drug addicts,
pickpockets or just plain tramps cast up for the night.
They are sleeping in Rain Baseras –
dilapidated night shelters with no space.
It's too cold in Delhi for the usual pavements
so tents go up opposite Gandhi Maidan in Chadni Chowk
and sleepers lie in tattered blankets shivering for the morning.
Not far, there's a permanent shelter
with broken windows that let in nippy winds
where cast-off quilts serve as raggy covers.

Timepass, a rag picker, kicks his neighbour in his sleep.

The sleeper doesn't mind, for the warmth he gives out.
At least there is sanitation, but not clean
says Masood, a limbless beggar from Badayan.
It costs 6 rupees for 12 hours – and I'm not alone.
The food is free at nearby Gurudwara Sisjang Sahib,
hot cups of tea and a solitary TV.

Govinda's left leg is broken and in plaster.
He looks downcast and complains:
the blankets are not washed – they smell
the toilets are not clean – they reek.
He casts a glance at poor Masood and, voiceless,
thanks the destroyer and creator Siva
for the part his *Karma* has cast him.
Soon he'll be back on Jumna's banks
letting out his line to hook the fish
that he might live in future transmigrations.

Ashraya Adhikar Abhiyan, NGO for the homeless,
runs this shelter – and 40 others.
We try to make the sleepers comfortable, he says.
Blankets and mattresses the government does not give us.
Neither funds – we have to cast about for money.
Each day is dicey and we are often driven to extremity.
We cannot do more than throw in our lot with them.

From hour to hour as the night advances
the temperature
drops
to
3

Instrumental

Dr. Vikas Gupta cradles the instrument of Moghul courts
His sitar, body of gourd
Teakwood face and neck
Seven steeled strings
Upper bridge copper and brass,
Under which:
Harmonic strings, thirteen
Tuned to the scale of the *raga*.

Mr. Shri Mahendra Shanker leans over
His two-tuned drums, tablas,
Big bass and small treble
Tops leather-covered, iron at the centre
Sitting together like husband and wife
About to converse
Or couples taking to the floor.

Miss Kanika Pandey embraces her tanpura
Its six strings – steel and copper –
Meant for rhythmic harmonies
Ascents and descents of the seven-noted Yaman
Or midnight mood of the five-noted Bageshri.

From the earth, like a fresh spring,
The first sounds of the sitar –
The *alap* – seem to form
Unaccompanied, pure, thoughtful.
The tabla taps and the *gat* begins
Fingers running to high and low
First bold, imperative, overriding
Then fading to an O.
The tanpura, like a shadow, follows

Drones a central note, octave and quintet,
Shapes the composition's path
The bounds of the sitar's embroidering
And the tabla's patterns.
Her triple notes of *Desh*, *Malhar*, or *Megh*
Shut out all else
That the sitar may breathe in the wind's currents
And the drums in rapport with him
May be rapt.

Airport Butterfly

Landed at Kolkata
we waited on yellow line.
In white it took flight.

Sheets

Arrived at three-star Kolkata hotel
after flight, we mark soiled sheets,
ring down for change,
this done routinely with new marked pair.

At Purilia in starless overnight
we see them spotted under dubious cover,
lie on top till first crows call
and wait for street cacophony.

In Santinikatan boarding is ascetic bare,
linen, like blotting paper, stained,
small slits and splits appear
mark of perpetual wear and tear.

Approaching Kolkata in slow-moving train
we see them spread out by railway track
stretched indefinitely beyond the line,
bright white sheets bathing in the sun.

After Execution

In Kolkata, I read of a bullock at bay in Mumbai,
one of a herd – twenty thousand "strong" –
headed for the abattoir at Deonor.
Bolting when unloaded, this bullock stood
cornered in a scrap yard
in a scrap with butchers badgering him
all New Year's Day.
Colonel J.C. Khanna of the BSPCA with pride surmised:
"He fought slaughter and Bakri-Id sacrifice,
and – like Bush – has managed to survive.
Now the animal's registered seven at our sanctuary.
He's got some bruises, but'll be fine out in the pound at Malad.
George, we 've called him, battling bullock of Mumbai."

I turn back to the front page and read of a man at Baghdad
stood on a platform before first call to prayer,
insults flung – and hanged.[1]

---

[1] Saddam Hussein was executed on 30th December, 2006.

Resting Place

Santosh Mondal of the C.C.T. tells me
they come from Barasat, Madhyamgram and Dum Dum
in costly hearses to bury their dead at Bibirat,
to this place of stones and plaques marked with fond words.
    I read:
        Deepu, thanks, you taught us about love.
            ma, baba, Buri and Buria
   Jojo, 1990 – 2005, we will never forget you. Ghosh family, Khidipur.
Some come habitually to pray, to weep over those, the flowers of
    their lives
or bring wreaths to crown memorial in memory.
In marble they are made and engraved. I read:
`Moti 8-9-2001` *Guddu 9-8-2001* `Jack and Tipsi` *Sarah and Milky*
not inscribed lightly like Dryden's cutting comment
Here lies my wife: here let her lie! / Now she's at rest, and so am I
but gravely meant like
`Valeria, Valeria, my treasured pet / Never,`
    `never, will I forget.`
"Some mourners return at anniversaries to honour their animal
    idols," Santosh says.
"*Compassionate Crusader Trust*, that's us.
We are open for service 24/24 in case.
You should see how they jostle for burial space.
You look surprised, sir, no need – we've served stars like
    Rudrapasad Sengupta,
and humble people too – housewives from Sealdah and fishwives
    from Balasore –
all 've bidden valediction to perennial companions, made their
    tearful adieus
leaving us to look after the garden.
Here Tollywood's Tapas Pal buried his Spitz
and this poor woman her Patna goat.
This one's a dog – see the inscription?

And there's a cat – now that's an epitaph and a half!
You'll find pigeons too with messages on the marble,
and even tiny mice given kindly tribute.
Cockroaches? No, sir, our grounds for burial are philanthropic
and, of course, hygienic."

Three Feng Shui Matters for Pinky Kapoor

Shanta Arora's brother is going bankrupt.
He owns a hall for banquets – for birthdays,
funeral breakfasts, business buffets and wedding parties –
but there's a backlog of clients' debts.
The dates they give for settling up
extend to further dates; promises are not kept.
What to do?
Mrs. Pinky Kapoor replies:
You say you have a cut in the south-east corner of the hall –
Not good for cash inflow –
that way you'll lose a chunk of money.
Shanta Arora: What to do?
I would say the south-east needs water and wood
the first for wealth, cascading as fountains do
lit up in submerged green – and water-bearers
housing gilled and colourful creatures, blue pebbles
sea shells, fresh plants (not faked) – they'll grow as wealth grows,
but wood there must also be
which when nourished will start to soar and make sure
your brother keeps his head above water.

* * * * *

At 10.45 a.m. you were born in late June of '89
a strong fire-person – easily inflamed.
Beige will balance that, as will cream and yellow, rust and white.
Water too – in blue shades – should encompass you.
Don't deal in hot reds, nor purple, nor peach,
but earth colours as above, and those that gleam metallically.
Deepika, do you know your best directions – the ones that
        presage fortune?
Look then high northwards

and southerly where the deeps lie
eastward to Siam's shores and to ancient Andaman.
Think not of going west, nor turn to it for gain,
but stay where Pinky is in this palatial city;
here indulge in chat that you may be charged,
seek out your snake, that you may be charmed.
In four corners you'll find him, in a quarter, a square,
a season, or in an *adda* [1] foursome on College Street.
But be sure you connect correctly professionally, or you'll
    overheat.
Settle on metal first which might be IT or PC
then water which'll see you into banking with HSBC.
You asked me to adwise.
It's for you to choose wise.

* * * * *

I am a lawyer and practice from my chamber in Kolkata.
Last Monsoon, I built a house – two storeys –
in a river suburb. Near the south corner I bored a well –
very deep – from which we draw to drink and wash.
Entrance is from the south-west where Hooghly flows.
Yet my practice lacks liquidity and is going down;
nor does my father keep well; his tummy keeps runny.
May I know the source of our problems?
From where do they spring?
Is the house plan well-thought through?
Or does it go against current Vaastu or Feng Shui views?
Sorry to say, Mr. Banerjee, you are without direction.
Water in the south is wrong, it's ruled by fire
which won't be quenched; nor does open water bode well;
so sink tanks deep to north or east
making sure to keep them sealed;
then tap pious power with a new way in,

not earthy south-west as you have put it,
the place peace should reign for residents,
but open where compass points and quivers;
then step over the threshold with blessings
like fresh-wed couples crossing to new chambers.
Such sound spirit will revive your sire and all your suits.
Thank you Mrs. Kapoor. I'll start rebuilding.

[1] Bengali: a form of intellectual exchange

Kumbh Filth

At Sangam where Ganga, Yamuna and mythic Saraswati meet
the Sadhus quiver in a chill wind before water.
Fog falls on bathing ghats as the Ardh Kumbh mela begins.
After month-long penance, pilgrims, priests and petitioners
come to be cleansed in the sacred river – and find it foul.
From Kanpur and Allahabad, effluence oozes into it
issuing from upstream leather works, affluence of gross owners.
Sadhus, water-standing, see the river stained and shallow;
they shout out for fresh-flush from near Narora Dam.
Expect not prayer and sacrifice in this defiled stream, one cries,
but a string of soiled suicides.

Tagore at Twenty-Five

"From the words of the poet men take what meanings please them; yet their last meaning points to thee" – *Gitanjali*

In a boathouse by Ganges he chose solitude
close to waters' murmurs, nature's songs,
wild ducks in autumn come from lakes in Himalayas
his company.
Dusk-furled sacred Lotus
will open to the east its hundred petals
bare holy honey to him
inscape, crest of understanding.

Times were when river turned ink-black,
star got lost, harp-string broke.
What inharmonious walls built then around him
plastered with dust and sand!
A dungeon in Rabindranath's name
shrunk from plunge into deep being
– dance, dream, and death.

Among tall grasses a maiden
came to float a lamp when west darkened:
dedication to sky.
Her timid flame, current-caught, swirls
– or so the young man thinks – into oblivion.
His lamp is blown out.
Subdued, he spreads his mat on boathouse floor
takes up harp – string mended – plucks out song:
strains of sundry kind to a singular silence;
feels fierce flood, sees full firmament
and there on the water – a carnival of lamps.

Tagore at Sixty-Two

"Had I not danced like a madcap myself, I could never have inspired the girls and boys to dance."

Cycle of spring songs with actors from Santiniketan
Poet and King discoursing on stage at Madan
with girls – beautiful as shrubs and flowers
especially Madhavi – blossom-white, sweet as lyre,
crowned. Round moon too with wreath as moonshine
and youthful Basanta Lord of Spring in fine
costume sings with boys to assembled instruments.
Then comes the Poet centre-stage bent
on dance in wild whirls with King,
gorgeous flora and spent spring
body gone in spirit to music, round and round
till Poet casts away his cap and King his crown
and Finance Minister grasps their hands
and audience thunderous apprehends
a lucid unity of hemispheres, and entranced
sees no cleft other in the dancer or the dance.

From Poverty to Palace

Smoke fills Kolkata air from roadside charcoal cookers.
I cough inside our taxi, stopped at long lights, engine off.
Stalls, plastic-canopied, are set up for trade in trinkets,
clips, candles, chocolate, crystal and crude craft.
Shacks are garbage-made – shelter for outcasts and refugees,
their shrine to elephantine Ganesha, colourfully garland-draped.
There's a bony old man soaping himself on the curb
water pouring from street faucet;
children go bare-footed, bent women sweep,
boy with box for shoe-shine squats,
cross-legged menders pick out minimal tools,
men drink sweet tea, eat puffed rice, sit for chat;
dogs lazy in deep day-dream – lights go green
driver switches engine quickly on – hoots, beeps, bells, bellows –
we roar forward to Dum Dum, terminal and flight.

Air is AC at Dubai, set at 20 and purified.
Glass spans space like Paxton's palace,
silver stairs move up as though to sky.
Water falls magnificently courtesy of Company,
concourse carpet – soft – as are waiting seats when sunk into.
Smart car – to be won – on sloping stand glistens with glamour
        girl.
No duty here at costly shops but logos mark wares up
as do brands with famous appellations, designer-written,
coffee shots with euphonic Latinate names
menus of blatant gastronomic subterfuge
gems and jewels announced with doubtful provenance
and bottled scent of dubious sense and smell.
All this I thought at first was paradise
until I saw the shallow in it – and at what price!
Now India's my incredible heaven, and this my empty hell.

For Sunder and Guilaine

There's a wedding mass
at Saint Mary's in Dubai
in warm winter
at the year's beginning.
The introit's sung,
the priest's uttering his dearly beloved,
his *Kyrie eleison*.
Bride and groom listen to a liturgy of love,
one which keeps no score of wrongs,
responds to the faithful zither player
and to the hopeful notes of the ten-stringed harp.
Acclaim them – the bride and groom – with Alleluia
before the homely homily is said
before the marriage rites are read,
the two as one are wed.
Blow your trumpets angels!
Blow into the round earth's imagined corners!

The Gospel's read, the Lord's spell is spoken:
one commanding no servitude,
no yoke, but a goodly resignation.
The priest's advice is spared:
reminder of love's fruit,
its cares, its charges, and acquittals.
Now two hands are rightly clasped
ready for declaration:
"I, Sunder, will not put you asunder."
"I, Guilaine, take you of all men."
"Thus pronounced, let not your vows be renounced!"

There's a peal as bells are rung
and rings of faith are fixed on fingers

echoing infinity in Holy Trinity
blessings of exchange.
Now comes thrice-happy rite to sup on
presaging co-mingled body and blood,
a transubstantiation approving Love's alchemy.
Thus consumed through consecration
let there now be celebration.
Let the guests grasp hands, grant peace to each
while in church vaults the choir's *Hosannas* sound;
and let the kettle to the trumpet speak,
the trumpet to the canoneer without,
the canons to the heavens,
the heavens to earth
in solemn proclamation!

Nile

A great artery
it runs at first fast
but by the desert slows to a meander
bifurcating to multiple veins, meeting upcoming sea, mixing with
    the tides
till expiration in the deep.

The ancients knew not from where the waters came
when in flood the river rose
fertilizing the sun-lit soil.
They thought the god mighty
to send so much to lands that saw no cloud,
knew growth only near the banks
with deadly waste beyond
– near and remote –
near rock-dead valleys,
remote where not even the dead could reach.
Surely the god was vicious to send such
voracious water creatures with the flood
to feed on unsuspecting folk
who to appease them offered sacrifice
that they might not be devoured by approaching inundation.

Nourished so, settlements after many floods took on high
    temples,
proud palaces, luxuriant baths, became cities,
chief seats, metropolises, centres of the painter-scribe
whose fashioning of funerary papyri
brought dead kings from their tombs,
and sculptors who might mimic a woman's stride,
a captive's cringe, a hippopotamus harpooned

in alabaster and fine limestone, or hard porphyry, basalt, breccia,
    granite
cut and lugged along the desert floor
shipped north from Tura or south from Nubia
to be crafted into perpetuity.

In such wise, the river vivified a dead land.

Hieroglyphic Picture

The eagle stands by the stand in the courtyard – bolt upright
The owl on the hill slope leans forward with loaf in mouth
The lion on the mat lies parallel to the water
The snake, like an unused lasso, coils up in the reed flowers
The cuoil chik chats, one foot in hand-woven basket
The horned viper, hidden, gazes from a folded cloth.

Pairidaēza (for Halim)

The Lord grants gardens their lease
of fruit and flowers, their weeds even
growing under olive trees.
The wonder of seeds and seasons,
of spraying, unfurling, and fading, follows
after toil on earth, a well is bored
and saplings are seated in moistened soil.
Nature answers to your creation:
building for their babes
birds find sanctuary here;
for this they break out in perfect song.
Bees gather where flowers sway
in the sweet breeze, and colour's augmented
by butterflies alighting. All lore is here
in this parvis, deep-laid in your design.

In this garden the Lord gives and takes away.
You come and pass through, live and pass on.
Your stewards are left collared, harnessed
to propriety; they give feed,
save the fig from aphid ants,
stop slug pilfer, pull out the thorn,
and at ripe time harvest.
This is no place of vaulting display
where people of moment are marked
as once in sovereign parks shah and vizier
entertained their own high-flown eternity,
but reclusive and remote in desert's depth
rich in soul's seclusion, and in solace
lightening the Lord's unbroken recreation.

Sticky Fingers

I am ordering Turkish coffee.
Cakes and pastries lie under glass.
I point at a decorative bun.
The waiter gestures me to take a closer look.

There is someone at my shoulder.
I see a hand stretch out, prod and thumb my bun
then lifted and licked.
"*Ruhe!*"[1] the waiter cries; the interloper drifts away.

"*Voyou*"[2] – and to me – "Take your cake and eat it, quick!"

On the sea front I extract the sticky thing
grasp where it has been thumbed
bite into its sponge, chew its gooiness.
Prompted by thirst, I remember the purchased coffee.
I hear a merry hoot and see on the promenade
a young man lifting a cup to his lips.

[1] Arabic: Go away!
[2] French: Loafer

Kuwait's Old Boats (for Claudia Farkas al-Rashoud)

There's a mud wall around the yard:
boats are beached, shark-oil coated, palm-frond sheltered from
    the sun.
Piled teakwood brought from Malabar shores will form new
    vessel's deck and hull,
fen asel – mast; *fen Ibrahim* – spars; ironwood branches cut from
    curved boughs
set along ship's keel – its ribs. *Qalalif* [1] tools bedeck the yard:
pliers, plane, chisel, capstan, adze, bow drill, hammer, saw;
made from Kerala coconut, cordage for rope rigging.

Craftsmen and artisans start early in the quick light;
master-builders stand with hands in deep *dishdasha* [2] pockets
housing shipwrights' ancient implements:
chalk and string for straight line on uncut plank;
fork-shaped stick – *galam* or divider – measurer of cut-wood
    contours
this for tight fastening to ship's ribs; triangle of brass – *hindaza* –
    protractor
with plumb bob – *zubild* or weighted string – to set up slope for
    stem and stern.

In the yard, children build small boats with scattered wood scraps
in imitation of their craftsman fathers; witness keel laid with
    expert eye;
teakwood oiled from dripping sharks dead on racks in the sun;
watch cotton, coconut-oiled, stuffed into cracks between
    planking;
mixed lime and fat coated below the waterline putting off heavy
    barnacles;
see caulked hull take the shape of finished ship.
These, ordered on trust by gulf pearlers, water haulers and ocean
    traders,

are measured in *mon* – large baskets palm-frond woven
    conveyance for dates.
They range in name and application:
Boom tishala bring building stones from desert quarry; short-
    distance *gatah*;
narrow rowing *ghauwas* and short-keeled *sambak* taken out for
    pearls
as are square-sterned *jailboot,* small *shoo'i* and sleek-swift *bateel,*
flagship of the pearling fleet. Fishers with their nets set off in
    foderi;
barrel-fitted *booms* head for Shatt al-Arab to take aboard fresh
    water –
supplementing waning wells – for donkey riders to vend from
    door to door;
tender *duba* serve as cargo-movers alongside three-masted *baghala,*
pride of merchant men built like Portuguese man-o'-war, with
    raised cabin,
stem, stern and poop carved decorously. Made from Malabar
    cotton
triangular mainsail fifty stitched widths; mizzen aft added;
set on protruding boom lashed to stem head – jib called *bumiyah;*
canvas for *shamandy* – mast stepped forward of the wheel to keep
    boat-balance;
and hard to hoist *gabiya* set aloft the main yard, thought by
    captains to lack utility.

New-made vessel sits on cradle ready to roll on slim poles into
    the water.
On that day, when noon tide is spring high,
carpenters start sawing at mat bags set under bilge
and as the sand runs out the ship leans slowly on her heavy hull.
Now captains labour at capstans, letting her out foot by foot
and in fresh *dishdasha* townsmen dance, thump on drums, sing sea
    songs,

clap hands with insistent vigour, they waiting for stern's splash
    into shipyard water.
Then wives will ululate and launching feast begin with fatted ox
    or sheep or goat
roasted in honour of Kuwait's new boat.

* * * * *

He holds a basket by its rim.
His foot's on a stone fastened to a rope twisted round his leg.
His nose is clipped.
Let go by the tender he drops deep-fathoms into the water,
is swept astern; tender feels the rope loose, hauls up the heavy
    stone
catches it with slippery hitch about the sweep,
takes the diver's basket line, slacks out, feeling for his slight tug
sign that his dive is done.
All the pearlers are down now.
Tenders hold taut lines leading aft to the sweep's round arms.
Still they are down . . . down . . . down . . .
. . . comes a pull – tender hauls in fast, hand over hand – and
    strong.
Head and shoulders break surface, basket first, and treading water
with raised arm, swimmer shields wide-pupilled eyes from stark
    light,
blows out air and water, whale-like, from his tortured lungs,
sea streaming over his shoulders, slips off nasal clip
and breathes in deep air.
Allah kareem! Y'Allah! [3]
Baskets are boarded, the men hoisted, oysters tipped out deck-
    scattered.
After five score breathless descents, tired divers crawl into
    corners and sleep
untouched by companions' sprawling limbs and aching moans,

or the lapping of waves on anchored boat. For months they've
    braved
contrary currents, water's weight and threat of roaming sharks
pearling in Kuwait-built boats off the southern shore
– Juleya, Ras Misha'ab, Kheiran and Az-Zoor –
but still must bear desiccated skin and hair, sore-swelled gums
    and body bleeding –
curse of seaman's scurvy – price of costly pearl.

          * * * * *

Sails are unfurled on big *baghala*, raised
to drumming, chant to Allah, dance,
deep growling song led by *nahhamah*[4]
high note for hands on yard and halliards.
The ship's away, first to Failaka to take on
salt, flour, rice, wheat, corn and dried *zubeidi* fish
for crew's humble sustenance.
Thence north to nearby Basra, or opposite to Gusba,
purchase cow or sheep, kill, cook and dry it for the crew;
load on dates for onward sale to distant India.
Nokhada's[5] business done, sail south length of Gulf,
through pirate straits into open ocean, course set for Karachi.
This is September monsoon time, north-east fair-wind friendly,
unless becalmed . . .

After long haul dates are traded in Bombay's port;
days later, docked at busy Calicut,
wood is bought and rope for boat; tamarind, rice, spices
(especially pepper), coconut, cloth, coffee, tea.
When all's boarded, *baghala* pulls away from harbour quay
for fresh sea search along Malabar coast.
At Mangalore roofing tiles are purchased and piled in ship's hold;
they'll be sold across the ocean, payment for mangrove poles
to be laid, at journey's end, as cover for mud brick houses.

The crossing to Barbary Coast is long:
accompanying *qalalif* builds small boat on deck
to profit at first African port of call;
he's here to mend storm-blasted mast or spar,
to swim under hull when damage is dire.
Seamen work on ropes and sails, weave and stitch
repairing them; others below bail out the bilge.
Some rest before their shift; one is sick.
Helmsman holds steady to *nokhada*'s course
arrived at by sightings, sextant, or dead reckoning;
he navigates by sight of stars at night.
Nahhamah keep company with rhythmic song:
the crossing to Barbary Coast is long.

Mogadishu comes into faint view on horizon's subtle curve.
The crew crave approaching land.
Sails come down at port entrance, one by one furled.
Lines are thrown out and caught for mooring.
Traders board with port officials.
Log book's reviewed, sick removed.
Sun sinks, darkness falls tropical-quickly.
In the wake of great distance *baghala* rests at berth.

There's singing in the harbour at Mombasa
talk in heterogeneous tongues
quay-side high-pitched calls
racket of cart and carriage, locomotive whistle.
Lamu logs, brought from palm-fringed green arm across the bay
by small white-sailed boats, paint the water red.
Among graceful bows and stately sterns
Kuwait's trader lays alongside the wharf, roofing tiles unloaded.
There's a heavy scent of copra at the customs house;
food smells pervade populated streets – catered tastes:
Swahili, Indian; Baluchi, Arab; Punjabi, Japanese.

Here's where crews exercise land limbs
join in short diversion, drink fresh water, take stock of sets, rips
    and rocks
in the course of ocean going.

Kept company by Irani *boom*, Omani *jailboot*, *kotia* from Calicut
    and local coasters,
Kuwait *baghala* full-sails south along palm-fringed shore, in sight
    of golden beaches,
by green Pemba island, wide of leeward reef, into channel set fair
    for port of Zanzibar . . .
With supplies aboard, they sail on to protracted days of danger in
    Rifiji Delta:
maze of waterways, capricious currents, crocodile and hidden
    hippopotami;
jungle-steaming swamp where mangrove grows, noxious vapours
    – nature rotting in the sun;
scum and mud – leech-tick propagated; giant stinging bee,
    pestilential gnat;
snake – fork-tongued poisonous – pressure-killing boa
    constrictor.
Fever takes a hold, rashes, infected sores afflict the men;
they drink infusions – herbs gifted by Kuwait's old ladies –
or gulp down healing water of boiled crabs.
In this untamed terrain mangrove trees send down roots from
    branches to meet the river;
they're impervious to it, inhospitable to water worms,
wherefore logs are cut laboriously, stripped of bark, piled into
    small boats,
hoisted to *baghala* deck for mule-like transport
and sale worth seaman's salt.

Late calls at Mozambique and Grand Comore
the ship's set due north for Ras Haifun

thirty-five-day haul to Somali shore
if not caught in calm or storm.
Thence along south Arabian coast with fair wind fading
past Muria and Masira Isles, through wicked Hormuz Straits
into safe home waters.

In Kuwait Bay small vessels set out to meet full-sail *baghala*.
There's song, vigorous clapping and dance on board.
Rowers sing with the rhythm of their oars.
The ship comes in, docks gently and sails are furled.
Instruments come out – cymbal, water jug, and double-headed
        drum;
lute, metal mortar – *uns* [6] merriment begins.
The seamen, with town in attendance, wash away in song the soil
of a nine-month passage: trade, tackle, trim and toil.
Yet ship duties are still not done:
culinary items offloaded and carried on strong backs to
        waterfront warehouses,
Eid [7] goats to market,
cloth for clothes and sails,
timber to furniture workshop or shipwright's yard,
frankincense for sale at *Souk*,[8] conjuring smoky essences.
Last comes large cargo: Rifiji mangrove poles dropped into the
        sea,
floated to shore, and stacked ready for the roofs of cool mud-
        brick houses.
Then rigging's taken down, gear taken off
and on high tide the ship's beached, hauled up and cleaned;
rats and roaches purged from hold, barnacles scraped off,
hull shark-oil-coated and left palm-frond-sheltered from the sun.
With ship shored up for long summer, the men receive their
        reckoned share:
they count their good fortune.

Epitaph

Fear no more the heat o' the sun,
The ships' long voyages are rightly done.
Pearls are past and sail no more,
Not gone, but stored in Kuwait's sea lore.

[1] Boat builder
[2] Man's white garment
[3] O Bountiful Allah! O Allah!
[4] Professional singers
[5] Captain
[6] Celebratory music
[7] Muslim holiday
[8] Covered market

Kuwait Eclipse

On that eve
a walkers' bridge came down
hit by a too-tall crane
on the Sixth near the trade fair site
sending a woman – at one hundred and forty kph–
to her death in the debris.
Cut off, cars crawled south
edging from lane to lane
in the fight to exit for Messila
– and when free of the freeway
drivers, on eighty-kilometre roads, home bent
pressed down on right pedals
setting off prohibitive bells
as, nodding, they tapped out numbers
into space, which bounced back to home phones
making connection with maid or man or minor.

There was convergence too: witness mangled metal
green light winking down hard shoulder
when not blocked by retarded cars impatient to pass
and blighted bodies in pools subtracted from family
ready for the stretcher.
This was no Immanent Will causing consummation,
not that, but vainglory such as addicts know
who thinking themselves inviolable from Newton's Law
try flying from a block – jump – and gravitate below.

On that night the moon shone round
before the Earth's shadow would encompass it
and it become a shadow of itself.
Full though the roads were, some as though in sway
careered breakneck down slow lanes
while in deep discussion others doddled in the middle

or drifted over glass eyes and silver studs
inching to their ruin with Maxima, Merc and Mercury
shaving past flat out.
Next came the late man who apparently in lunar pull
and flagrantly in four by four
putting his foot hard-down at the red
smashed transversely into innocents
wiping them and him off the Arab map
in conflagration.

The cool moon reflected on the waste,
on the detritus of speed
on the witlessness of doomed youth's
passing of bells: invitation to slaughter.
No mockeries now for them, no call to prayer,
nor any voice of mourning, but wailing from weaving van
en route for Casualty:
no transfusion in the field's confusion
but a drawing-down of blinds:
on the pallor of girls' brows
on the moon's face which, like a shroud,
from left to right was slowly covered by a curve
(Earth amid its satellite and that whose satellite it is)
till darkened seemed a spatial ball suspended in the black
covered now, covered by the world's shadow
like a shroud, like a shroud.

4th May, 2004

Cultural Crossroads

In England when you walk the street
You look down towards your feet
Or up to grey and rolling sky
But surely not in someone's eye.
It's different when you're at the wheel
When traffic's so thick it seems surreal,
Then you look at others and indicate directly
expecting them to acknowledge you correctly.

Vice versa in Kuwait: you'll be watched as you walk
And if you're a girl he'll likely start to talk,
Want to know your mobile phone
And even ask to visit you at home.
On the other hand, when he's in his car
Be it Nissan, Ford or high-powered Jaguar
He'll come fast and furious onto the Fifth Ring
And drive as though he's not seen a thing.

Two Limericks

There was a young student of Kuwait
Who would always arrive at class late;
    She would look at the time,
    See it was nine
And forget that her class was at eight.

There was an old man from Kuwait
Who swallowed a large fat date.
    Then he felt a great pain
    Until up the pip came
But alas, it was 'ready too late.

Animal Matters

In Salwa's Cooperative shop they screen pictures
of lions stalking antelope in the African bush;
rodents running from swooping eagles are swept up
like shopping from supermarket shelves.
You can see wolves in packs hunt down deer,
vultures hover for the pickings;
zebras are stripped by lean leopards
then gorged in a furore of gore.
I turn away from it
and head for the sliding door.

Chivalry in the Age of the Chevrolet (for Nasser)

He saw me walking in the Kuwait rain
One wet winter evening after writers' workshop
The buses stopped for the unlikely flooding
The heavens having unloaded everything, it seemed,
And inundations that Gulliver might not have matched
Had he drunk sixty hogsheads of Lilliputian wine.
I put down my umbrella and with wet feet
Tumbled into his lucky limousine
Thereby falling into a felicitous friendship.

Another time he saw me and my tribe on the road
Waiting for our bus in the blistering afternoon
Our shades up against the angry sun
And inviting us in to his cool conditioned draughts
Plus the powered luxury of his automobile
Drove us to town.
We'd meet him then at home or *diwaniya*[1]
Take the kids to action movies
Bite into burgers on the beach
Or picnic at his Doha nursery
Where plants and trees sprung up under his protection.

There came a cat to our flat door
Mauled by lewd males and catapulting kids
Lay hid in a corner as though to die
Until taking nourishment she settled in nicely
Legs stretched munificently sprawled on our floor
Amid my tribe's rompings and ravings.
But this was a lodging which could not last
She being of the tiger breed
And could not but petrify our luckless mice
Clawing one mortally when the door was down

And the house was out for cleaning.
Then came our knight and bundled her
Scratching into his big boot
Drove her to the sanctuary of his farm
– A big game park for our Tiger.

A knight he was in mighty steed
When seeing Merc or Ford or Dodge hard-shouldered
And drivers peering peevishly under raised bonnets
Their cars like steaming nags on heartless asphalt
He'd stop – and with chivalrous calm
Breathe life into moribund metal.
Or when men squabbled on the roadside at some affront
Be it bump on back or scratch on wing
Or one had dared to eye another's wife
While stopped at long lights
He'd pull up if the parties had taken to punching
Pull them apart to stop
Fists and feet turning bloody.

There came a pup to our ménage
As fluffy as an unshorn sheep
As active as an ant
With ears that flopped foppishly
And eyes as dark as depths
One September birthday.
Notwithstanding ubiquitous stains and pools
On cared-for carpets and shining tiles
We could not be parted from him
Our *Falafel*,[2] our dear dog.
But come the summer
And departure for vacation in cool climes
The prospect of Britannic quarantine
And hard-felt separation

We knew not whither he should go
Our compatriots too having taken flight
For pleasant strand or Disneyland
Mortgaged homes in temperate zones
Or Buddhist prayers in Himalayas.

Then came our knight in shining Chevrolet
To fetch our dog to his Doha garden
For him to range the bitten grass
To laze under spreading branches
Scent out wild smells
Romp with strange dogs
Chase cats up trees
Cock ears at rare birdsong
Or eye snakes surreptitiously in the fissures
Of gnarled walls or cracked earth.
So spent he his first summer
– In an original garden
A pup's paradise before the Fall.

[1] 'Parlour' meeting, usually a group of men.
[2] "Fluffy," but *Falafel* (a ball of fried chick-pea paste) to Arab ears.

On My Way to the Bank

I heard a hiss and a "Mister!"
turned, and saw a large car crawling forward
past the Kaifan bakery. The driver beckoning,
I approached thinking he might be lost.
"Mister, you have a kind face," he said
and I smiled at that. "I am Saudi.
You are from?" and I proffered *Ingeltra*.
"Well-cum," he said though he was not from this place.
"I have no money, Mister, please help me."
His *dishdasha*[1] was summer white,
his hair uncovered, a well-groomed wavy black.
"You have a kind face," he pleaded.
I didn't smile – and he went on – "Engine not working,"
though I could hear it purring perfectly.
"Car need maintenance, money"
– with which I mentally turned out my pockets.
"You help me," he smilingly seemed to assume,
but the beautiful beige of his limousine, its shining chrome,
leather luxury, its massive dashboard strewn with flickering light
left me unimpressed by his so-called plight.
Now he could see that my kindness was wanting
for I pleaded no money. "You have two faces,' he said
and taking hold of the wheel with his manicured hands
he screeched into the maelstrom of the morning's traffic.
Out of sight, I went on my way to the bank.

---

[1] Man's long white garment

Siamese

I heard it mewing in park bushes
pitifully, not like those that inhabit this place,
silent, untouchable, darting like tigers for their prey,
but lost in a wilderness without nourishment
nor any sanctuary.

I saw it creep out uncertainly
its blue eyes dazzling in the daylight,
stare at me, someone not seen before,
and with expectant gaze warm
to my tentative stroke.

Dumped, I thought, by midsummer travellers
vacating Kuwait's oven sun and winds of sand,
the cat left, like chip packs, in the grounds
swept and tended by the Bangladeshi men
where the wild ones roam.

There's a worker there to whom I say good day;
he sometimes stops his sweeping
to bend and touch them and they, wild though they are,
respond with high tail, rubbing of legs
and purrs of perfection.

To him I tried to speak; he smiled
with broken teeth, I beckoning him to follow.
He saw my Siamese, reached out and gathered him up
from the lonely path like a lost child,
his arms a cradle.

I came back in the morning, anxious for the cat,
wanted to know if he'd been found and claimed,

but, no, there he was, silk hair bedraggled,
the park keeper, an Egyptian, telling me brokenly to take it.
"Come," he said. "Finish!"

I went home without him, conscience torn, not wanting
a new pet chapter – of feeding and bathroom litter trays
and the search for a refuge in the fast-approaching holidays.
So laden, I saw a stick-leaning saint speaking in a London park,
Mandela at ninety.

Chastened, I went next day on my early walk and found it
fed by the Bangladeshi man with scraps on silver foil,
bones kept from a humble hostel meal. He smiled
broken-toothed at me, happy with his eating cat,
I passing by.

Again I saw him, this time sweeping dust into the morning air.
I could see no cat, nor scraps, and his wretched face was straight.
He put down his frond as I stopped to ask.
"Outside," he said, a glance at the iron gate. "Cat gone"
– and swept past me.

I rued the Siamese, thought of him thirsty in strange streets
lapping at soaped car water, hungry at house bins
or running under fast wheels, losing his last life,
as, after breakfast, I stepped into the empty bath and with flannel
scooped out stray ants.

Mass at Salwa

The singers lift up their voices
In faith of Father
Refuge in Son
Protection by Holy Spirit.
Thrice sung, thrice said, thrice signed
What do these reiterations signal
My mood distraught with doubt
My pettiness all-powerful
My mind in pieces?
The apolytikion is chanted
The Gospel Introit started
The boys bear candles to the altar.
But I hear no harmony in it
No lesson in Apostolos nor Epistle
Nor see light in a flicker.
The deacon may call *"Dynamis!"*
But I feel no charge
Am incapable of supplication
Can offer only paper on a plate
Think wanderingly without wonder.
Do the Angelic Orders follow invisibly
The singers of the Cherubim hymn?
Has the chalice been made full
The gifts consummated
The lamb broken into four?
But I am unprepared
Stay seated; I have not heard
Inward words of invitation.
But here's a girl with a basket of bread.
She's smiling and stretching – offering.
I take a piece and taste
– gone, gone, gone is the waste.

At Last in Kuwait

Among strung trunks, boxes, bags, strapped pictures, mirrors,
fat mattresses leaning lazy against soiled walls,
dead screens cloth-covered – PC and TV –
IKEA shelves, new-bought, lined up in their packs
and AsIs dressing table – minus mirror – unpadded as yet,
bins and baskets – all plastic and filled,
sofa disassembled, arms locked, lining in tatters,
cushions buffers between breakables
tight-rolled rugs, fishing rod unfirm and awkward to pack
hospital crutch, non-returnable, easel packed in pieces
dust-free curtains, sun-faded, clean in sealed black plastic;
scissors, sticky tape, string, screwdriver on scratched top
of glass-fronted cabinet for sale at knock-down price
as was washer that went for a song, Gibson fridge,
fuse-switching stove (of make unknown), too-heavy sideboard,
armoire, weak-hinged, with doors falling,
ample desk at which I drafted these weekly for workshop,
accrued for *Poems of the East* and *After-Images*,
we – Thérèse and I – survey the aggregation of eighteen years
packaged for Hawali lorry soon en route
through two kingdoms, Ba'ath country, to Bekaa' and Mount
      Lebanon.
We have the final papers – *laisser-passer* for the load,
contract terminated, disconnected phone, last rent paid, power,
      water,
permission to reside stamped *cancelled*, identity annulled.
In the remaining detritus we slide into nonentity.

Borrowed books are rarely given back.
I have two to be returned before departure
but the lender – not seen for years – can't answer:
home phone's *rakam ghalat*,[1] mobile's out of the coverage
      area.

What to do but pack them with the others for the road
and when shelved at journey's end remain reminder of my sloth.
In reverse, I'm after a large volume, *Great Short Stories of the World*,
one of mine unread, loaned long ago to a lecturer friend
not seen nor heard for a term or two. I ring . . .
and she's busy marking finals papers; I ring . . .
and she's taken up with external examiners; I ring . . .
and she's having coffee with them at the *Café de l'étoile*
in the country's prime shopping mall.
"I'll meet you both later," she says, "at the place where they're
    staying,"
and, as an afterthought, "I'll bring the book."
We had wanted to spend the last night as at first in Kuwait
in hotel hedonism, but with backs sore and packers still packing
that plan makes way for a night on the floor.
We are game any way for a drink in the foyer (non-alcoholic of
    course),
to talk to Doctor Lee about her passion for Vikings and Norse
and shy Doctor S (no card) who's researching Shelley – Percy
    Bysse
while Chekra – she's handed me my book – sits politely quiet
relieved, I guess, at term's end and externals' flight tomorrow.
So with heavy book and lightening hearts the last drive to a home
half-emptied, half-familiar, to a last sleep – on half a bed.

It is summer and departures are plentiful;
foreign workers – Egyptians, Indians, South-East Asians and
    Caucasians –
leave for annual break or, like us, one way passage at contract's
    end;
a few perhaps for deportation; others set on brief business;
locals on weekend jaunt to Beirut, Dubai, or Sharm el-Sheikh
or towel-wrapped for *Umrah*.[2]
Lamees, Fudda, Fahad, and Razzuki are here for leave-taking,
    friends made warmly;

we sit uneasily at Starbucks, pass last words, hear a call to the gate,
exchange farewell embraces . . . wheel our cases to a long line.
Nasser, our knight, has come too for a final adieu.
He sees us make slow advance in the curling queue;
he is talking to a smoking official who has nothing to do;
our knight calls us out; we follow his finger to the first-class
    entrance;
we hesitate, catch on, and heave our bags away from the waiting
    passengers.
The smoking man gestures us to be quick through the security gate;
I fumble with loose change, stray paperclip, watch; load luggage
    onto the belt;
Now through, we turn and wave our thanks to Nasser for his *wasta*;[3]
    he smiles
and we, passing through first class, at last feel like true citizens of
    the State.

[1] Wrong number
[2] Pilgrimage to Mecca
[3] Favour or influence through connections

At Ortaköy

There's a church that's now a mosque
by the waterside where Bosporus Bridge crosses.
Two minarets rise above an old cupola
topped by gold crescents – on the dome too
where once a cross was.
Set into its four walls, Corinthian columns
worn by Black Sea winds
the vapours of passing vessels
constant pigeon droppings
and all that's gone by since Byzance times.

On this and the other shore
more minarets, and somewhere synagogues
couched among the houses; and churches
with bells that ring for rest
still standing for worship.
At Ortaköy I heard a call to midday prayer
echo over the water
as tugs and tankers passed
from south and north
and ferries crossed from west and east.

Coming Home

We are on our way to England, Thérèse and I,
landed at Istanbul waiting now for our connection.
There's a notice in red for passengers to Madrid, Paris, Tel Aviv and
      London
telling us to stay in line for check in at the transfer desk.
There's a bunch of settlers —families on their way to the Promised
      Land —
dressed like Puritans, early migrants to America;
tourists in casuals — shorts, jeans, tight skirts, and T shirts in bright
      colours
with rucksacks, scuba diving gear, and boots slung over tanned
      shoulders;
suited men on business travelling light with their laptops;
Gulf expatriates guffawing, inebriated, bent on holiday;
women, long-skirted and scarf-covered, their cute kids hanging on.

There's a call in English for a Hebrew speaker;
a man bound for Tel Aviv is questioned at the desk;
a settler falls out and volunteers; they let the passenger pass;
the queue moves worm-like forward, security men interrogate;
they've picked out an Arab woman with a ticket for Tel Aviv;
"You are going to Israel?"
The woman nods.
"Why?"
In an American accented English: "On vacation."
"Why Israel?"
"To stay with family," she says looking into the official's eyes.
"But you are a citizen of the United States" – and holds up the
      woman's passport –
"Why are you going to Israel?"
"Palestine," she says.
The official looks nonplussed for he knows nothing of *Annakba*.[1]

I look back as we pass through to wait for the call to the gate
and wonder . . . hope . . . imagine . . . her going home.

Epilogue

At Stansted, we took our luggage off the belt, Thérèse and I,
and headed for the green door. But someone had been stopped:
a woman in black down to invisible shoes, head covered,
her case undone on the Custom's table, an officer removing the
        contents one by one:
blouse, skirt, wrapped packets, petticoat, stockings, night dress,
        knickers,
and like Lawrence with his snake, I thought how paltry, how vulgar,
        what a mean act!
Felt so, I passed through sliding doors to the bus and a troubled
        journey home.

---

[1] Arabic: "Catastrophe," referring to the Arab/Israeli war of 1948 when many Palestinians were driven into exile.

Acknowledgments

"To Have and To Hold" has appeared in *Earth Love* 34 (February 2010).

"At Sheba" in *Poetry and Audience* 45.2 (Winter 2010).

"Desert Flowers" in Caroline Sullivan, *The Path Not Taken* (National Library of Poetry, 1996), and *Earth Love* 40 (2011).

"After Execution" in *Dial 174*, 81 (Spring 2010).

"Three Feng Shui Matters for Pinky Kapoor" as "Three Feng Shui Matters" in *Weyfarers* 109 (December 2010).

"Siamese" as "Cat in Kuwait" in *Weyfarers* 110 (May 2011).

"At Last in Kuwait" in *The Journal* 33 (Summer 2011) and *EEK* (Ex-Pats E-Magazine, Kuwait) June #2, 2013.

"Rachel in Rafah" as "Rachel in Rafah, Gaza" in *The New Verse News* 16th March 2012. http://www.newversenews.com/ and in *DesertPeace* 17th March 2012. https://desertpeacewordpress.com/category/poetry/

"Not Far to Galilee" in Earth Love Sponsored Poetry Climb (to Ben Squlaird). 6th July 2012. http://www.youtube.com/watch?v=c36q0lFVurY/

"Trio" in *Weyfarers* 112 (August 2012).

"Hieroglyphic Picture" in *Morphrog* 7 (July 2013). http://www.morphrog.com/morphrog7/Antony%20Johae.html/

"Cultural Crossroads" in *EEK* (Ex-Pats E-Magazine, Kuwait) February #1, 2013.

"Arrival at Rafik Hariri International Airport" in *The North* 50 (2013).

"Tōhoku and Fukushima" in *Poetry Space Summer Showcase* June 2013.

"Dr Hu's Last Words" in *Quarterly Literary Review Singapore* 12.3 (3rd July, 2013) http://qlrs.com/issue.asp?id=46/

"Music for Two Players" in *Poetry Space*. Autumn Showcase – September 2013. 29th August 2013. http://www.poetryspace.co.uk/2013/08/autumn-showcase-september-2013/ and in *Poetry Space Autumn Showcase* September 2013.

"Black Gold" in *Weyfarers* 114 (October 2013).

"Skating in Kuwait" in *London Grip New Poetry*. Autumn 2013. http://londongrip.co.uk/category/poetry/

"Kamishibai" and "Going Hawaiian" in *Poetry Space*. Winter Showcase – December 2013. 28th November 2013. http://www.poetryspace.co.uk/2013/11/winter-showcase-december-2013-2/

"Throwing Stones" in *The Transnational*. 3 Mar. 2014. http://www.the-transnational.com/throwing-stones.html/

"Creation Story" as "Chinese Creation Story" in *Ariadne's Thread* 10. Theme Issue: Mythology (2014).

"Mosque in Kabul: Epilogue" as "Mosque in Kabul – 2002" in Stephen Boyce, Pam Job and Judith Wolton, eds. *so too have the doves gone: reflections on the theme of conflict*. Wivenhoe: Jardine Press, 2014.

"Diviner" in *Weyfarers* 115 (August 2014).

"At First in Kuwait" in *London Grip New Poetry*. Autumn 2014. http://londongrip.co.uk/2014/08/london-grip-new-poetry-autumn-2014/

"At Shiraz" in *The SHOP* 46-47 (Autumn 2014).

"Tagore at Twenty-Five" and "Tagore at Sixty-Two" in *International Journal of Culture Studies and Social Sciences* 2.1 (2015).

"Arab in a White Steed" in *Orbis* 172 (Summer 2015).

Biographical Note

Antony Johae (b. Chiswick, Middlesex, 1937) spent from 1945 to 1955 at preparatory and public schools. He failed "O" level GCE English Literature. In the late 1960s, he was fortunate enough to train as a teacher and in the 1970s studied for his BA in English and European Literature. He then went on to write his doctoral thesis: a comparative study of Dostoevsky and Kafka. In the 1980s he taught English Literature in Ghana and Tunisia. He married Thérèse, from Lebanon, in 1985. In the 1990s and the first decade of the new millennium, he taught English and Comparative Literature in Kuwait. His articles have appeared in international academic journals. Antony has been writing poetry since the 1970s. Some eighty poems have appeared in poetry magazines, anthologies and online in the last five years. *Poems of the East* is his first published collection. Others are soon to follow.